THE Mellotron Book

Library of Congress Catalog Card Number: 2001088666

Publisher: Mike Lawson
Art Director: Stephen Ramirez; Editor: Patrick Runkle

236 Georgia Street, Suite 100
Vallejo, CA 94590
(707) 554-1935

Also from ProMusic Press

Music Copyright for the New Millennium

Also from MixBooks

The AudioPro Home Recording Course, Volumes I, II, and III
Creative Music Production: Joe Meek's Bold Techniques
Professional Sound Reinforcement Techniques
I Hate the Man Who Runs This Bar!
How to Make Money Scoring Soundtracks and Jingles
The Art of Mixing: A Visual Guide to Recording, Engineering, and Production
Music Publishing: The Real Road to Music Business Success, Rev. and Exp. 5th Ed.
How to Run a Recording Session
Mix Reference Disc, Deluxe Ed.
The Songwriter's Guide to Collaboration, Rev. and Exp. 2nd Ed.
Critical Listening and Auditory Perception
Modular Digital Multitracks: The Power User's Guide, Rev. Ed.
The Dictionary of Music Business Terms
Professional Microphone Techniques
Sound for Picture, 2nd Ed.
Music Producers, 2nd Ed.
Live Sound Reinforcement

Also from EMBooks

Studio-in-a-Box
The Independent Working Musician
Making the Ultimate Demo, 2nd Ed.
Making Music with Your Computer, 2nd Ed.
Anatomy of a Home Studio
The EM Guide to the Roland VS-880

ProMusic Press, Mixbooks, and EMBooks are imprints of artistpro.com, LLC

Printed in Auburn Hills, Michigan
ISBN 1-931140-16-2

About the Author

Frank Samagaio

Frank Samagaio has been a musician, multi-instrumentalist, composer, arranger, and Mellotron enthusiast for over 35 years. He owns a 16-track studio where he produces and records projects for himself and other artists. Most recently, he revised and updated the service manual for the Mellotron Mark II. Frank lives in San Diego, Calif., and is the owner of Mellotron M400 #908.

Dedication

This book is dedicated to Leslie J. Bradley (1916-1997).

Foreword

Rick Wakeman

The first time I saw a Mellotron was in 1968 at Morgan Studios in North London. It was "quietly" sitting in a corner minding its own business as I arrived to do an organ session for producer Tony Visconti. I asked the engineer what this strange looking piece of furniture was and he said it was called a Mellotron (a Mark II) that had arrived a couple of weeks earlier, but nobody could keep it in tune, so they just used it to put tea and coffee on.

The session over, I hung around and asked if I could play with their new giant coffee table. "Help yourself" was the reply, and two hours later, which was when I was chucked out, I had managed to work out how to keep this strange sounding instrument in tune...oh, and also how to reset the tapes when they came off of their rollers and spilled out the back!

A few months later I received a call from Tony Visconti to say that David Bowie wanted to use a Mellotron on his new single and I was the only person he knew of that could keep the machine in tune so would I like the job. I said yes, went along to Trident Studios in London and recorded "Space Oddity." There was a write up in some newspaper about it and suddenly I was the Mellotron session player in demand!

I used them on the Strawbs album *From The Witchwood* and when I eventually joined Yes, I bought six of them!

I suppose it can be safely said that my relationship with the Mellotron has been a real love-hate one. In truth I love the unique sounds they produce but at the same time have been genuinely reduced to tears by them when they frequently misbehaved whilst out on tour. Truth is though that perhaps I really should never have sold them off when I did, allowed four to get stolen, (including the classic custom-built double manual) and should have one again, at least in the studio and maybe even out on the road, hold on, what am I saying!

The true facts of rock life are now cast in stone. The Mellotron will go down in rock history as the instrument that, alongside the Moog synthesiser, played the most important part in giving keyboard players the musical colours they always yearned for. OK, there was a technical price to pay, but boy, it was worth it.

Anyone got a Mellotron going cheap? I think I'm about to go retro in the studio.

Rick Wakeman
November 2001

Foreword

Mike Pinder

My association with the Mellotron has been a love affair that started in the early sixties. From the first time I set eyes and ears on the Mellotron, I was captivated by its unique sound capabilities. After working at Streetly Electronics, the manufacturer of the Mellotron, I had the opportunity to introduce it to people around the world during my years on tour with my group, the Moody Blues.

The unique, lush sounds that the Mellotron enabled me to create always brought forth inquiries from the audience. "How do you make that sound?" It gave me great pleasure to present these sounds to so many people and create Mellotron Magic.

Please enjoy the following account of what was history in the making.

Mike Pinder
October 2001

Contents

Introduction

Did you ever have an experience where you came across someone or something that made an indelible impression, an impression that has stayed with you since and won't let go, sort of like Richard Dreyfuss in *Close Encounters of the Third Kind*? That describes how the Mellotron has been for me. After talking to other Mellotron enthusiasts, I found out I was not alone.

My own story began in early 1968, driving home late one night from a club gig at a naval base in Imperial Beach, California. These were the budding days of progressive FM radio, and the strains of the full LP cut of the Moody Blues' "Nights in White Satin" came on. Mesmerized, I thought, "Wow, what a sound." Little did I know what it really was. I bought the LP *Days of Future Passed* and, subsequently, *In Search of the Lost Chord*. Reading the credits and looking at the latter LP's photos, I reasoned that the referenced "Mellotron" must be that strange keyboard Michael Pinder was seated at. I still didn't realize what it was at the time.

Fast forward a few months to November 1968, the day before Thanksgiving. The Moody Blues were playing at Grossmont College. I was bummed because the girl I was looking forward to taking canceled at the last minute. Giving the spare ticket to my best friend, we went in search of the lost concert. I was a bit upset to find this same girl at the concert with a bunch of her girlfriends. The first band, Framework, a local product, was very good. The next act was the original lineup of Spirit, who were great. During the Moodies' set up, I saw drums, two guitar amps and an "organ," and the buzz was that these guys had better be good or they were going to get booed off the stage. For the life of me, I cannot remember the first song they played, but hearing the sounds of Michael Pinder's Mellotron Mark II live was my *Close Encounters* experience. There are the same goose bumps on my arms as I write this. I quickly forgot about the girl.

I attended six out of seven Moodies concerts here in San Diego during the '70s, focusing on everything, but particularly the Mellotron. For unknown reasons, I have few photos of Michael's Mark II even though I had a good camera rig with me at each show.

At San Diego State, working in the band's administration office during 1971, I was able to find out about and contact Mellotronics in London. Peter Nichols wrote me on several occasions outlining that my beloved Mark II was no longer made, as was the 300, and that the only available model was the 400. No resources, no money, just a burning dream. I arranged with Dolph Rempp and Ken Berry of Studio Instrument Rentals in Hollywood to come up and check out their Mark II. Upon arrival on a cold and rainy December evening in 1971, my drummer and I were greeted by a mass of tape spaghetti, as someone earlier that day had tried to change stations while still holding down the keys—Ouch! In the summer of 1973, I revisited that same unit, which had now acquired a coat of white paint, but was operable, and spent several hours in my first hands-on experience with a Mark II courtesy of Ken Berry. (Please, can I take it home with me?)

Move ahead to 1978. From an ad in the *Rolling Stone* classifieds, I contacted Jim Herbst, then in Norman OK, who sent me Polaroids of a mint condition Mark II with an asking price of $3,000. His partner, Dennis Meehan, wrote me a week or so later to say that the Mark II was dropped to $2,000. Times were tight, and I had to pass on it—hindsight tells me I should have done whatever I could to obtain it. Haven't most of us been in that position before? Over the years, Jim had two others, one for $3,000, and one labeled in "pristine" condition for $5,000. Bill Eberline, formerly of Sound Sales, then of Crest Audio, offered one to me with a cache of spare parts for $3,800 in 1985. I again passed because I didn't want to cause friction in my marriage. Now I feel like Sidney Greenstreet's character in *The Maltese Falcon*: "You can always get another wife; there's only one Mellotron." Some of you have been there before, too.

There were several conversations to gather information with the late Leslie Bradley in the early '80s. He was very accommodating and a hell of a nice guy; it's nice to know that there will be Mellotrons in heaven. Conversations followed with Dominic Milano at Contemporary Keyboard magazine, Frank Levi of Yes/Night Owl Music in New York, Dolph again at S.I.R. in Hollywood, who termed Mellotrons in general as "junk" and told me to get it for what little I can. I had contacts with Jim McNeely of Mellotron USA Ltd. In New York in 1983 and 1985 inquiring about getting a 4-Track. I'll always remember attending the Winter NAMM show in Anaheim to see the Digital Mellotron I was promised would be there and finding an empty vendor's booth. Add to all this various occasions where I had the opportunity to pick up a 400 for between $300 (with a brass capstan) to $700. Does any of this sound familiar to Mellotron enthusiasts?

Things remained dormant until early 1997, when I discovered the Mellotron websites. Since then, I have had the wonderful opportunity to become acquainted with a number of Mellotron owners and enthusiasts too numerous to mention, and had the privilege of revising and editing the *Mark II Service Manual* for Mellotron Archives. It also caused me to relapse into Mellotron fever, renewing my pursuit for ownership of a Mark II. Some day, Lord willing.

While expanding on my personal collection of Mellotron photos, it struck me that there's never been a formal book specifically dealing in Mellotrons, compiling the historical data on the company, the models made, dates, timelines, people, etc., just piecemeal information on various websites and the occasional book or magazine. After toying with the idea of using some of the unique photos I had obtained in a millennial Mellotron calendar, postings on the Mellotronists mailing list yielded positive grass roots support for a book project. After all, don't we already have enough books about '59 Les Pauls and '58 Strats? Isn't the Mellotron worthy of a similarly dedicated book? Doesn't the Mellotron deserve its rightful place in music history alongside these other classic instruments? The obvious answer is yes, and you, dear reader and Mellotron enthusiast, are about to enter a world where the most pleasing sounds last for eight seconds in real time, and forever in the mind's recorder.

Projects such as this are not a one-man venture and require the assistance and cooperation of a host of individuals. Alas, memories fade and become altered with time, however, I have been fortunate in being able to contact key people in Mellotron history, along with valuable input from fellow Mellotron enthusiasts to piece together the most comprehensive Mellotron work written to date. I would like to extend special thanks to my agent, Arthur Fleming, publisher Mike Lawson and editor Patrick Runkle of artistpro.com, Martin Smith and John Bradley of Streetly Electronics, David Kean of Mellotron Archives, Bill Eberline, Jim McNeely, Jerry Korb, Michael Pinder, Ian McDonald, Rick Wakeman, Wooly Wolstenholme, John Wetton, John Hawken, Tony Visconti, and the too-numerous-to-mention Mellotron artists, owners, and enthusiasts who responded to my requests for interviews and information. May your tapes never break or stick.

CHAPTER 1

The History

The Rise, Fall, and Resurrection of the Mellotron

Special thanks to David Kean and Mellotron Archives (www.mellotron.com) *for extensive contributions to this chapter.*

The history of the Mellotron, which now spans six decades, has had more than its fair share of ups, downs, twists, and turns, much like a good mystery novel.

The Chamberlin

In 1946, while playing his home organ, a clever man named Harry Chamberlin got out a portable tape recorder to record himself playing for some friends. After having made the recording, he came upon the idea that if he could make a recording of himself playing a whole piece, he could also record himself just playing one note. Then, if he could build a machine that was capable of playing back these single-note recordings on demand, he could record and reproduce the sound of virtually any instrument. Harry had envisioned the first sampler, and this idea culminated in the original Chamberlin units, which eventually evolved into the Mellotron.

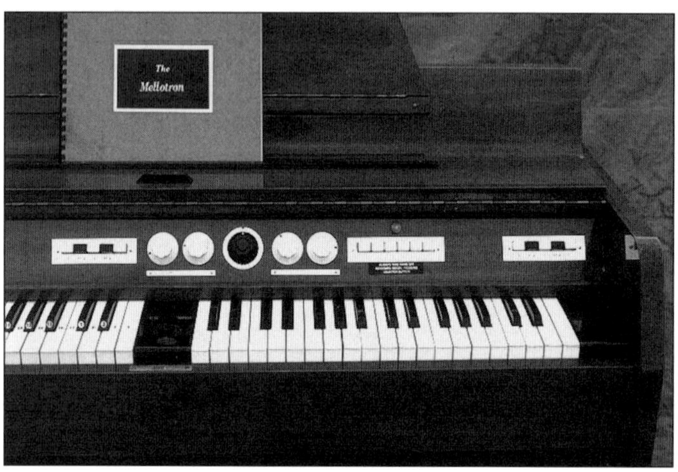

Photo Credit: Mellotron Archives

Mellotron Mark 11 #23. Owned by David Kean.

According to Harry's son, Richard, Harry's first machine was the Model 100 Rhythmate, built in 1952. This machine had 14 loops of drum patterns and was aimed at the home organ market. Pleased with the success of this machine, he then built a shop in Upland, Calif., and began production of the Model 200 keyboard (MusicMaster 200). This instrument used quarter-inch full track tape and the first version of his multi-station tape changing system. Oddly, this machine also had a steel subframe that was soon abandoned with the design of the 300/350 series. This lack of a subframe was the major design flaw in all of Harry's subsequent models up to the M series. It's the first thing that the Bradley brothers would add to this design in producing their first Mellotron.

Harry then built the remotely operated Model 300/350 (two separate cabinets) and the organ style cabinet model 600/660 MusicMaster. These machines used 3/8" tapes and had 35 keys, G to F. Harry felt that this range was enough to cover the usable range of most instruments and still left room in the cabinet for another 35-note keyboard that had "combo" rhythm tapes and special sound effects. The 3/8" tape afforded him more sounds and a proprietary tape format that insured tape sales. This was a largely successful design, and in 1960, Harry set up a shop in Ontario to build and sell these instruments.

After a period of time, Harry hired a man named Bill Fransen as a salesman to help him increase sales. Bill was very good at his job, but there were two big problems: Harry's inability to keep up with the orders, and the basic unreliability of the mechanism. There were six banks of tape in each keyboard that scrolled from "station" to "station," thereby giving the player a different set of three sounds to choose from. His method for stopping this scrolling had about a 40 percent failure rate and caused tape disasters few have ever seen the likes of. Also, the replay heads he used were unmatched, producing a very uneven playback from key to key.

Nine months later, Bill concluded that even though Harry's wonderful keyboard was sound in principle, he was never going to fix the problems that continued to plague the tape shuttling system. Believing that the idea was too good to be left alone, Bill "appropriated" two of Harry's Model 600 MusicMasters and took them to England to try to find someone with the engineering and manufacturing talents to bring this idea to fruition.

The Mellotron Is Born

In 1932, Leslie Clifford Bradley started a British engineering firm, which his three sons joined as they left school. They made a variety of products that included, during World War II, machine tools for the manufacture of Spitfire and Lancaster aircraft. After the war, Leslie and his sons—Les, Frank, and Norman—continued as Bradmatic Ltd., electro-mechanical engineers, only a few hundred yards from Aston Villa football ground.

In England looking for interest in the Chamberlin in 1962, Bill Fransen contacted Les Bradley and asked if they could supply a set of 70 matched replay heads. Bradmatic had been manufacturing magnetic erase/record/replay heads since the 1950s (designed by Leslie C. Bradley), and also manufactured two-speed tape recorders (3 3/4 and 7 1/2 ips) under the Bradmatic name. Les consulted with his brothers Frank and Norman, and replied that they could indeed do this. The brothers were very curious about this strange request (Frank rightly guessed that the heads must be for some sort of music machine) and inquired further.

The brothers were impressed when Bill showed them how their 70 replay heads were being used, and when Bill asked if they could improve upon and mass produce this machine, they gave him an enthusiastic "yes." According to John Bradley, Les just stood there, and couldn't believe what it was—such an incredible concept to use magnetic tape in that way. It didn't work that well, and was noisy, particularly when it cycled. The sync tape (for the cycling system) actually had holes punched in it, and a pair of contacts had to touch each other through the holes to stop the machine. Needless to say, this was not very reliable, and the circuitry was such that it couldn't decide which way it was going, so it would start cycling backwards and forwards, banging through the reverb. But it proved the point that the idea would work. The sync tape on the Mellotron Mark I, II, and 300 would have a recorded block pulse of 1,000 cycles. Les couldn't sleep that night because of all the music that was going around in his head; he was excited about it.

The Bradleys ended up building their own versions of the machine with backing from bandleader, radio celebrity, and entrepreneur Eric Robinson, as well as magician David Nixon. Mellotronics, the firm Robinson created for the purpose, recorded quarter-inch master tapes in London, and Bradmatic converted them into the unusual 3/8" format they had saddled themselves with in borrowing the Chamberlin design, using a double-decker tape transport that Les Bradley and Eric Horton invented and developed. It was a fixed-speed machine, dubbed the "Mothertron" by Dave Kean of Mellotron Archives. The tapes produced at the original Streetly factory from 1962 to 1986 were all made on this machine. With the advent of the M400, Mellotronics decided to have its own tape copying setup in London (these are machines now owned by Mellotron Archives) so there were two sources of Mellotron tapes.

If you are able to compare original Streetly and London tapes in, say, a Mark V, you will find that they are out of tune with each other! Anyone with a Mellotron that works will know that pitch variations exist between the various sounds available, not to mention the pitch variations within the same sound. It gives the machine character and the player nightmares. John Bradley says, "If you compare an older tape set to one of today's available from Streetly or Mellotron Archives, they'll likely be out of tune with each other." Consequently (subject to the above variations), all tapes now available from Streetly come at the "Mothertron" pitch of original Streetly tapes. They can, of course, supply them at London pitch if you require.

David Kean of Mellotron Archives relates, "this tape recording process was a daunting task. Consider this: For the rhythm side, they needed 35 tape recordings of a rhythm section playing in time, in tune, and each tape had three of these recordings across 3/8" in tape that had to start at the same time. Multiply this times the six "stations" that were selectable, involve stretching tape, and the fact that it's 1963. No digital editing. No synchronized tape lock. Just a lot of head scratching and a stubborn will to make it work. It took 13 weeks to record, edit, and sequence the first master set of Mark I rhythms and fills. The lead sets were next to be recorded because Harry's leads, only intended to be used on the right-hand keyboard in a prototype demo machine, were not in tune with the Bradley-produced rhythms. Remember, one capstan drives both sides of the machine."

Once the recording was done, they went into business and did quite well. The Bradleys at this point believed that the idea was Bill's and that he had registered the patent for a tape replay instrument in the UK. They had no reason to believe that they were infringing on someone else's patent or intellectual property. Les became suspect when Bill wasn't able to cite technical specifications relating to the machine, and eventually found out that it was Harry Chamberlin's patent. Les then invited Harry to England. When the dust settled, Harry agreed to a settlement from the Bradleys for a sum of £30,000 in 1966. Harry reluctantly shook Bill's hand and went back home to continue his own path, which culminated in the Chamberlin M series of the 1970s.

Meanwhile, in late 1962, prototypes of the new instrument were called the Franson, with no accounting for the spelling change. However, the name wasn't used. John Bradley (Les' son) believes that the name change to the Mellotron

Photo Credit: Streetly Electronics

Bill Fransen posing next to the first production Mellotron Mark I cabinet, before the keyboards had been fitted.

was Bill's idea, a hybrid of melody and electronics (originally "Mellotrone," noted on Bill's early paperwork). Production went on in the newly converted factory in the Midlands town of Streetly, near Walsall, under the Bradleys' control and with Bill Fransen's assistance. The Simplex tape heads used on the Mellotron head blocks were designed by Bradmatic, manufactured by another company in Birmingham, and then purchased by Bradmatic for installation in the Mellotron.

The Mellotron Takes Off

The Mellotron rapidly became a huge success, with its unique sounds outweighing its sometimes poor reliability, its bulk, and considerable expense. The Beatles (particularly John Lennon) were said to be total Mellotron converts, although reportedly George Harrison's Mark II originally belonged to Brian Epstein, and there is no record of Ringo Starr having ever owned one. The SFX Mark II was purchased at auction from Abbey Road Studios' "Sale of the Century" by Mike Oldfield in 1980, and was eventually obtained and renovated by Streetly electronics; it was subsequently sold to Paul McCartney. This is the Mellotron used by the Beatles on the White Album, and not the "Strawberry Fields Forever" unit as commonly believed. More recently discovered studio records indicate that this latter unit was rented for the "Strawberry" sessions.

The Rolling Stones got in on the act as well ("2000 Light Years From Home"), and a whole new genre of music sprung up, fueled by bands like King Crimson, Barclay James Harvest, and the Moody Blues. Incidentally, the Moodies' keyboard player, Michael Pinder, had worked at Streetly for 18 months before going professional and featuring the Mark II as his main instrument. Michael's job there was to play the finished Mellotron at the end of the assembly line and make any final adjustments before it was sent to the customer. He fell in love with the sound and decided that it would be an ideal addition to his new group, the Moody Blues. Leslie Bradley helped Michael purchase a used Mark II from the Dunlop Tyre Factory's social club, and the group promptly used it to record their first hit single, "Love and Beauty"(recorded 7/17/67; released 9/22/67).

The Beatles cut "Strawberry Fields Forever" (released 2/13/67 in the U.S., 2/17/67 in the U.K.) is perhaps the most instantly recognizable use of Mellotron flutes. However, according to "The Mellotron Story" (BBC Radio 2 Program, 1997), Graham Bond was actually the first to use the Mellotron on a pop record; "Baby, Can It Be True," performed on *Ready Steady Go* in 1965, precedes both the Moodies and the Beatles.

By the late '60s, the Mellotron sound was on its way to becoming a sonic archetype in our pop music consciousness. Mellotrons were never going to be a really mass-market instrument, but they were carving out a vitally important niche for themselves. All Mellotrons are based on the principle invented by Harry Chamberlin, where each key simply sets a length of tape in motion, playing back whatever was recorded on the tape. They were thus the predecessors of sample playback machines.

Creating custom Mellotron samples wasn't impossible, either, but this generally involved recording what you wanted and sending it to the Mellotron factory to be converted into a rack of tapes for your machine. Some 15 years before the Fairlight, there was a prototype Mark II Mellotron that could record onto some of the tapes on the left hand keyboard. The parent company, Mellotronics, was very nervous about this because they were already having trouble from the Musician's Union, so the machine was taken to pieces and never saw the light of day. There was also a 1/4" conversion kit available for the 400 that enabled you to record and use your own quarter-inch tapes. In a foretaste of how samplers evolved, early Mellotrons would have a bank of backing tracks and percussion tracks, like loops today, as well as multi-sampled lead/chordal instruments. You'd even get little bursts of applause or other ambience on some of the tapes—including Bill Fransen's 'Yeah!' at the end of the Dixieland rhythm track.

Kean continues, "The development paths taken by Harry Chamberlin and the Bradley brothers went in two different directions. They both knew that they needed to improve reliability, portability, and make a larger choice of instrument sounds available."

Chamberlin abandoned the multiple "station" idea of shuttling the three-track tape for new sound selections and instead changed to 1/2" eight-track tape with stereo playback capability. This was the M series. The M-1 was a single 35-note keyboard. The M-2, or M-1D as it was originally called, had two keyboards; a 25-note keyboard was added to the left of the 35-note one. The M-4 had 4 keyboards, and the Riviera model 800 had 2 M-2 style units in one cabinet and a fifth foot-operated 25-note unit. This last machine was Harry's crowning achievement and is now owned by Mellotron Archives. Richard Chamberlin remembers only two of these units being built, 4 M-4's and 5 of the M-2's seeing the light of day. The production numbers for the M-1 suggest between 100 to 300 units were produced between 1970 and 1981, and it is arguably the best sounding instrument of this type.

The Mellotron evolved in a much different way. After many calls to make the Mark II more portable, the Bradleys designed and built the Model 300 Mellotron. This unit (the oddest of the bunch) hints at the direction that would lead to the M400. The 300 had one 52-note keyboard, quarter-inch tape, and no pitch control! Only the first 25 units had this much-missed feature; afterward, it was available as an option. Imagine a Mellotron that one couldn't tune. The tape library was completely redone for this instrument, but only 60 units were made.

They realized quickly that even though the 300 was a much slimmer version of the huge Mark II, it still wasn't portable enough, and the sounds available still didn't satisfy the thirst for more variety. To satisfy this demand, the Bradleys also abandoned the multi-station platform, but retained the proprietary 3/8" tape format. They then developed a removable tape frame or "cassette," and expanded the original Mark II library to include another 16 new instruments that were deemed more "necessary," i.e., the 8-voice choir. The new instrument designed to use these new tape frames was the popular M400; you couldn't go to a progressive rock concert in the '70s without seeing its unmistakable profile. It was also usually the only white keyboard on the stage. At 122 pounds, this smallest Mellotron sold over 1,800 units and was the only design that came close to being a marketing success, in terms of the number of units sold.

Photo Credit: Streetly Electronics

Eddie (left) and Ivor producing Mellotron M400's at the Streetly factory.

The relative success of the Mellotron did not, however, render it immune from some degree of controversy. The popular myth is that the Musician's Union (UK) attempted to blacklist the instrument on the notion that it would put able-bodied session musicians out of work. In January 1967, however, the Musician's Union put out a statement to the effect that the Mellotron was no greater a threat to a musician's livelihood than that of an electronic organ. An authority no less than Michael Pinder appeared before the Musician's Union, demonstrating how he was using lead sounds on both keyboards, with no rhythms or fills, and in essence, broke their argument that musicians were being put out of work. Musicians were paid for making the original recordings, which became the intellectual property of Mellotronics, a practice no different from that of an artist hiring session musicians for a commercial recording. According to Mellotron historian Sarah Angliss, the Mellotron was banned for a short time only by the Musician's Union members working at the BBC, as part of a limited industrial dispute. However, in "The Mellotron Story," Edgar Froese commented that one British venue would not let Tangerine Dream perform with their Mellotrons unless they paid a large, up-front, and unspecified amount of money.

In 1971, Mellotronics was approached by Bill Eberline, sales manager for Dallas Music Industries (DMI) in Mahwah, New Jersey. (Dallas Arbiter was DMI's UK distribution arm.) DMI wanted to act as worldwide distributors for the Mellotron. Bill had previously worked as sales manager for Sunn Electronics, working with such groups as the Who. This distribution deal was done, and sales did pick up substantially from 1973-75, with Streetly unable to produce new units fast enough to keep up with the demand. DMI/Dallas Arbiter did not, however, honor any warranties on parallel-import Mellotrons from the UK. One Mellotron owner reported having to pay $54 in 1973 to replace a track selector shaft that was likely broken during shipping.

Bill Eberline stated that he had found workmanship problems on virtually every Mellotron shipped from the UK (cracked lids, skewed motor mounts, cabinets out of true, among others), and felt that Mellotrons were over-engineered. While these units were in perfect working order after leaving Mellotronics, they were never built to be roadworthy, and the associated problems were likely incurred during shipping. Bill emphasized that his main concern was quality control, and would make four to five trips to Mellotronics every six months or so to address these issues, but felt they were never heeded. It was also at this stage that the SMS2 servo motor controller was developed by Mellotronics to replace the less-stable CMC4 and CMC10 controllers.

End of the 'Tron Era

In the meantime, however, other products picked up by the parent company, DMI, were not doing so well. Disaster struck in 1976 when Dallas Arbiter (UK), suspected of questionable business practices and owing Mellotronics approximately £80,000, collapsed and eventually brought Mellotronics down with it. Bill Eberline had left DMI prior to the collapse.

In a devastating liquidation blunder, the inventory and the rights to the name were sold to an American firm that had been servicing Mellotrons, but not manufacturing them. According to John Bradley, Streetly had contacted the liquidator, informing him of his active role in manufacturing Mellotrons and his desire to keep the name. After promising Streetly that they could retain the name, the liquidator sold the rights to the name to an associate of Bill Eberline's. According to Bill Eberline, he contacted Peter Nichols, sales manager for Mellotronics in London, regarding the DMI bankruptcy and the trickle-down effect on Mellotronics. Along with a silent partner from Glasgow, Scotland, he met with solicitors with a briefcase full of cash and purchased the Mellotron name and inventory, which included the master tapes and tape cutting machines.

Streetly Electronics (having also been Mellotronics Manufacturing, part of the Eric Robinson Organisation, and also Aldridge Electronics for a short time) barely survived this collapse and continued to build Mellotrons. The Bradleys had to start afresh with a new name for their product, after losing the rights to the Mellotron name in all the legal wrangling, and eventually came up with "Novatron."

Bill Eberline then formed a company called Sound Sales to sell Mellotrons and tapes. It was located in Sherman, Conn. Concerned with providing a consistently better and more reliable product, the motor controller evolved into the SMS3, and Allen-Bradley potentiometers, gold plated contacts, and new parts were made and/or used that could be used to retrofit older Mellotrons. There was also the acquisition of a new Ampex tape-cutting machine using surgical blades from the UK; however, when the blades got dull, there was an occasional ripple on one side of the tape. According to Bill, he had even consulted with Les Paul on the recording of new Mellotron tapes. Bill claimed that no new tapes were made, and that customer orders for new tapes were fulfilled using the master tapes acquired from Mellotronics.

Kean continues, "All of this led to an unusual and somewhat confusing situation: Streetly would build a Mellotron, call it a Novatron, and sell it to you for $3,500. Sound Sales would take shipment of that same machine, call it a Mellotron, modify it, and charge you $4,500 for it."

According to Bill, by 1979 Sound Sales was building complete Mellotrons, the last unit shipped being one made from solid oak for Ann and Nancy Wilson of Heart. M400 cabinets in oak or teak, and the "M" logo on the back, were available options priced at $525 when M400's came in for servicing. However, this claim of Sound Sales building complete Mellotrons has been widely refuted, particularly by John Bradley. Many believe the first completely U.S.-made Mellotron was the 4-Track, initially conceived as an M400 retrofit kit.

Sounds Sales' locations (basically Bill Eberline's residences) in Connecticut changed frequently, moving first from Sherman to South Kent to Cornwall Bridge, then finally to Southbury in late 1979 and early 1980, where the company was affiliated with Bomar Fabricators, with Bob Kinney as company president. There, they developed the prototype for the Mellotron 4-track, with its 1/4" tape format.

By 1983, in the aftermath of a tough divorce, Bill had stepped out of the Mellotron picture. To this day, he is insistent that his concern was quality, and that he had no intent of taking the Mellotron out of Streetly's hands. Bill was pleased to learn of the care and love provided by John Bradley and Martin Smith of Streetly Electronics in restoring Mellotrons to the quality instruments they really are. He also believes that he still technically owns the rights to the Mellotron name, and would gladly return that distinction back to Streetly. Assuming that Bill still possesses the contract/notarized papers, without a legal transfer of the name to subsequent companies (e.g., Bomar, Mellotron USA/Mellotron Digital, Mellotron Archives), it would appear that pursuit of this claim would no doubt open a huge can of worms.

Enter Jim McNeely, a musician who had been working with major artists and Mellotrons in the '70s. Between 1983 and 1990, he spent $3,000,000—raised from non-musical investors, in a limited partnership, who were impressed with the concept of the Mellotron—to bring the Mellotron back as a viable product. The Mellotron 4-Track was produced at this time, all of four units, and has been dubbed "the Dangerous Maytag" due to its cabinet construction of extruded aluminum and sharp, unfinished edges within the internal mechanism. According to Jim, the "concept was problematic in that the smaller tape width didn't allow enough tape surface for the pinch rollers to grip, thereby causing traction problems." He also stated that no new tapes were made, that they worked from the existing masters, but did begin looking at creating new sounds, particularly different vocal/vowel sounds.

A name change was inevitable, and the company became Mellotron USA Ltd, located in Port Washington, New York. The company began to look for methods to retain the Mellotron tape sounds and began to explore the then-upcoming digital realm. A research and development branch was set up in Clearwater, Florida, as Mellotron Digital, with Chuck Fedonsak as its chief engineer. The New York office became Mellotron USA of New York. Tom Piggott, formerly of ARP, was also involved in the project.

Investors put $250,000 into developing a digital instrument akin to the Fairlight and Synclavier synthesizers. The VSLI chip was developed by Motorola and used in the prototype for the Mellotron Studio Symphony, which was to be priced at $25,000. The idea was to use a straight record/playback concept, and make it MIDI-capable without a lot of MIDI features. This was definitely not a road instrument. A smaller version of the digital Mellotron, the Symphony Grand, was to be priced at $3,000, and a prototype was featured at one of the COMDEX shows. There, it impressed the likes of master Mellotronist Michael Pinder, and at the 1986 NAMM show, there were lots of orders for the new instrument. After an attempt to go public in 1987, the stock market crashed, and the new company went with it. The only units produced were the prototypes, and the existing orders went unfulfilled. The company, however, had enjoyed its biggest success in producing MuArt 2- and 4-port MIDI interfaces, with the Tandy Corporation (Radio Shack) as its largest account.

Meanwhile, Streetly went out of business in 1986 after heroically bucking the synthesizer's domination of the market for four or five years. The Mellotron's big advantage over the synthesizers of the time was in their polyphony and the comparative fidelity of their sounds. Later on, they also managed to put up a good fight against early samplers, first by providing better fidelity, and then in the size of their 'memory'—you would have needed a then-impossible amount of onboard memory to have sampled an equivalent amount of sounds on a digital device. Okay, you couldn't re-trigger the sound until the tape had rewound (less than 1 second), but the seven or eight seconds the sound lasted for was a cut above the Emulator and Mirage—not to mention Akai's S700 and Roland's S10. (As a relevant aside, some people claim the possibility of making the sound of any one note on the Mellotron a little brighter and louder by pressing down hard on the key, a sort of primitive polyphonic aftertouch. However, no less an authority than Leslie Bradley says that this would only have happened on an instrument that was so badly out of alignment that the overall signal-to-noise ratio would have been poor.)

All Mellotrons had at least two and usually three tracks side-by-side on the tape for each note, and all the earlier models also had six sets of tracks one after the other on each tape. You could make the Mellotron fast-forward or rewind to get to the bank you wanted. While the technology to do this was a vast improvement over the Chamberlin, it still had its problems, particularly with the 300 (static problems, flimsier tape sticking to the tape separators, etc.). Other problems concerned the difficulty of building a motor that wasn't prohibitively heavy or expensive, but still had enough torque to cope with maintaining speed when suddenly, say, eight tapes were engaged for a big chord.

The factors that eventually sunk the legendary Mellotron were manifold: its unwieldy weight and bulk, its comparative unreliability once it was subjected to the rigors of gigging (particularly in having to withstand changes of temperature and humidity in being loaded and unloaded at venues), and its inability to manipulate sounds as a sampler could.

In 1986, Streetly went down and an era ended. The Bradleys had a complete card-index system for the Mellotrons, with details of owners, service notes, and so on, but very sadly this vanished during the factory sell-off when they went into liquidation. Appeals to music business celebrities to rescue the firm went unheeded.

Rebirth

Three or four years went by before a groundswell of interest and enthusiasm from Mellotron fans like Martin Smith and David Kean and musician/producers like Mitchell Froom built up, and meant that these wonderful dinosaurs of the electronic music world were not going to be allowed to become extinct.

Mellotron Digital's assets and inventory of Mellotron parts and master tapes were acquired in 1991 by David Kean, and subsequently became Mellotron Archives. Amongst its treasures were a solid oak and solid rosewood 400 SM, which stand 3" taller than a standard 400. A few years after acquiring Mellotron Digital, David, together with Markus Resch, started producing the Mellotron Mark VI, a further refinement of the 400, in limited numbers. This breaks tradition with the previous models in that the "Mark" designation was used for dual keyboard instruments (i.e., Mark I, Mark II, Mark V). Tradition would have designated this new model as a Mellotron 600.

In 1991, Les and John Bradley were approached by Martin Smith regarding his desire to acquire a Mellotron Mark II. Les recalled that the Moody Blues still owned a couple of Mark II units, and with Les' assistance, Martin eventually acquired Mellotron Mark II #219, formerly owned by the Moodies' Ray Thomas. From that meeting, John and Martin, while sharing a pint or two at the local pub, discussed the idea on numerous occasions for an album featuring the Mellotron. These meetings were also the genesis for the resurrection of Streetly Electronics. John (who worked at the factory from 1976-86) and Martin are hard at work servicing and rebuilding Mellotrons at Streetly Electronics, as well as producing new tapes, tape sounds, and tape frames. At this writing, Streetly will soon be producing a limited number of "roadcase" Novatrons, the T-550.

In 1993, *The Rime of the Ancient Sampler—The Mellotron Album* (Voiceprint VP141CD) was released, with tracks written and performed by a selection of Mellotron heroes and fans: Matt Clifford, Bill Nelson, Michael Pinder, Patrick Moraz, Gordon Reid, Sheila Maloney, Blue Weaver, Derek Holt, Nick Magnus, Wooly Wolstenholme, Ken Freeman, Martin Smith, David Cross, Chris Taylor, David Kean, Julian Colbeck, and David Etheridge. The CD also includes an extremely amusing taste of the 1964 Mellotron demonstration disc. Unfortunately, as of this writing, *Rime* is out of print, and Voiceprint has no current plans for a reissue. Also at this writing, however, there are plans underway for a second Mellotron-inspired and featured CD, with a projected release date in the coming months. (For more information on this CD and how to submit a Mellotron-featured song for consideration, see Ken Merbler's website at **www.tronsongs.com**.)

Thanks to Peter Forrest and his book The A to Z of Analogue Synthesizers *for additional contributions to this chapter.*

CHAPTER 2

The Principle

How the Mellotron Works

Application of Tape to Musical Instruments

Before Harry Chamberlin, there had already been several attempts at using magnetically recorded tape to supply the basic tones needed for electronic organs. They were usually variants of the endless loop system, and met with varying degrees of success. However, the continuously driven endless loop has some serious drawbacks if the full possibilities of recorded tape are to be exploited.

One of the attractive features of the recorded tape system is that the sound of a musician playing a note on an instrument is available and not an electronic synthesis of the same tone. It is obvious, however, that a musical sound is identified not only by the pitch and timbre of the sound, but also by the way in which it starts, or is "attacked." On the continuous loop system, this characteristic start is not available because there is no way of knowing at what point of the loop playing will commence when the key is depressed. Thus it would not be feasible to try to reproduce a piano or guitar by an endless loop system.

This objection is even more serious when we consider the reproduction of recorded rhythmic patterns, that is, a group of instrumentalists playing bars of rhythm accompaniments which can be used in conjunction with the other recorded instruments. In this case, it would be impossible to know at what point in a bar the rhythm would start and one would not be able to play in time with oneself.

Taking this into account, it can be seen that what is required is a system where the playing of the tape can be commenced from a known point. The Mellotron, by having a system where the recorded tape shuttles back to the starting point immediately after a key is released, has been designed to meet these requirements.

The Mellotron System

The following description is excerpted from the Mellotron Mark II Service Manual (revised and edited by the author), reprinted by permission from Mellotron Archives. A copy of the manual is readily available from Mellotron Archives at **http://www.mellotron.com.**

The front and rear storage rollers are prevented from moving by being coupled together by a chain drive, which also is coupled to the drive motor and the synchronized switch. The rollers can only move when driven by the motor.

A magnetically recorded tape is slung between the two storage rollers in such a way that about 6 feet more tape is allowed to hang than is required to stretch simply between the storage rollers. This slack is taken up in two loops passing around a system of pulleys formed by the top roller and the front and rear bottom rollers. The bottom rollers are pulled down by the tape return spring and thus the tape is kept tight.

Mounted above the tape is a key, which carries on its underside a pinch roller. When the key is pressed, the tape is squeezed or pinched between the pinch roller and the capstan. The capstan is a round bar that is made to rotate in the direction of the arrow at a constant speed. Thus the tape is made to travel towards the rear of the machine at a constant speed by the action of the capstan. Since the rear and front storage rollers are not allowed to move, the tape falls in free folds into the tape storage box, whilst at the same time the length of tape absorbed by the pulley system is reduced. This means that the bottom rollers rise as the tape is used up until finally, when the rollers reach the limit at the top of their permitted travel, a length of about 6 feet of tape has been played into the tape storage box. The dotted line shows the tape in a position near to the end of the playing action. If at this point the key is released removing the driving force on the tape, the pull of the tape return spring acting on the lower rollers will remove the tape from the tape storage box and pull the loops downward until the tape is tight again.

Since the rear roller has not moved throughout this action, it is clear that the part of the tape that was over the capstan when the key was first pressed, is now back exactly where it was before, ready to be played again.

Also operated by the pressing of the key is a pressure pad, which forces the tape into contact with the reproducing head. Thus when the above action is considered, it can be seen that the signal on the tape can be played from a selected point, this point being returned to as soon as the key is released. Since, as we have said, the slack tape taken up by the spring loaded loops is some six feet in length, then this is the length of tape available for playing. At the tape speed of 7 1/2 inches per second, the time for playing is about 8 seconds, which is adequate for most purposes. When 8 seconds is up, the key is released, the tape returning almost immediately to its starting position, after which the full 8 seconds is possible again.

Photo Credit: Jerry Korb

Mellotron Mark I #124 with internal frame lifted out for cabinet refinishing.

In order to increase the number of different sounds that are available, two things have been done. Firstly, three tracks have been recorded side by side on the tape and provision made for the head to be moved sideways to lay the desired track. Secondly, the tape has been divided longitudinally into six sections and a system arranged whereby the actual piece of tape stored in the spring-loaded loops can be selected. This process is known as cycling.

Cycling

In the Mellotron, there are six positions, or stations, to which the tapes can be set and taken together with the three tracks on each tape, and this means that there are 18 different sounds that can be replayed from each tape. It can be seen that this system gives a wide degree of flexibility because the exact instant on which a tape will start is available. So it is possible to play the tape from a point just as the hammer strikes the string of a piano or just as the guitarist releases the string. Similarly, a tape can be played starting exactly "on the beat" at the beginning of a rhythmic phrase.

The Mellotron uses two keyboards of 35 keys each placed side by side. The right hand one is a normal chromatic keyboard that can play two octaves of 18 different sounding instruments. A few examples are Clarinet, Flute, Piano, Guitar, and so forth.

The left hand keyboard controls the rhythms and orchestral backgrounds or fills that are used to accompany the theme played by the right hand. There are 17 different chords that underlie each rhythm, the chords chosen being those most commonly used by popular music. For example, if we make a selection to play a waltz, then any rhythm key which we press will commence to play a 3/4 tempo beginning on the first beat of a bar, but with different underlying harmonies, depending on the actual key pressed. In this way, we can alter the harmony played by the rhythm section to satisfy the requirements of the melody being played, while maintaining a steady rhythm.

The fills, which for the most part are played in octaves with the rhythm section, match the rhythm in harmony and tempo.

General Arrangement

The instrument is built in two halves on a basic metal framework. The top portion of the framework carries the major components while the vertical member holds the tape separators and tape return springs.

There are two similar keyboards, the right hand being used for the lead or solo instruments, and the left hand used for the rhythm accompaniment and fill section. Except for the split head block on the left hand side, both sides are identical.

The tape crosses the reproducing heads immediately after leaving the storage loops. The lateral motion of the head block is controlled by the track selection switch.

The track selection mechanism is mounted on a standard self-canceling push-button frame. The positions selected by the individual buttons are determined by the angle to which an adjustable plate, mounted on the track selector arm, is set. When the button is depressed, the track selector arm moves on its pin until the adjustable plate is parallel to the flat rear end of the push-button shaft. Thus the track selector arm will take up a position determined by the adjustable plate.

There are three tracks on the tape and for the lead instruments we may wish to select any of the three tracks or mixtures of two of them. The same is true of the fill section of the left hand side, but we can never mix rhythms. For the reasons outlined before, therefore, we use five-button frames for lead and fill, and a three-button frame for rhythms.

To press the tape into contact with the reproducing head, a pressure pad mounted above the tape is used. This consists of a felt pad mounted on a shaped arm, which is riveted to a light spring.

The capstan is in the form of a round bar running the entire length of the instrument and is the means by which the tapes are driven at constant speed over the reproducing heads. The capstan runs in ball races, which are mounted to the frame in special housings, and it is driven at the left hand end by the flywheel. The flywheel is, in its turn, driven by a belt from the capstan motor, mounted below the frame on the motor mounting board.

The tape storage box is constructed of wood and is supported behind the capstan on blocks screwed to the motor mounting boards. The tape passes through the box, adjacent tapes being separated by aluminum dividers that locate in slots in the back and front of the box. The lid prevents the tapes from rising out of the box when the tape is being played.

Cycling Motor and Chain Drive

The chain drive is used because it is essential that the front and rear rollers stay in exact synchronism. That is, if the front roller pays out 10 turns of tape, then the rear roller must take up 10 turns of tape, otherwise the difference would alter the amount of tape in the storage loop. The cycling motor is a shunt wound DC motor with a 30:1 gearbox on it.

The speed of the motor when cycling the tapes is about 150 rpm. Also driven by the chain is a unit called the synchronized switch, which enables the station selector control system to locate the correct stopping point. The slack in the chain is taken up by the tensioning jockey mounted under the bar that supports the keys. The keys are manufactured from seasoned soft woods, which are chosen for their resistance to warping. The white notes are covered with Ivorette (Trade Name) and the black are formed by plastic moldings glued onto the wood. The keylock is a device to prevent inevitable damage to the tapes if they were played whilst the instrument was being cycled. It is obvious that by playing a tape at the constant speed of 7½ inches per second, at the same time that the cycling was carrying the tape at 36 inches per second, can only result in severe and almost certainly permanent damage to the tapes. The device consists of a moveable bar or flap, which can be tilted by a linkage pulled by a solenoid. Only when the flap is in such a position as to prevent the keys being depressed, will it close a microswitch enabling the cycling operation to start.

Sound Control Panel

All the inputs are connected to the wipers of their respective potentiometers. The mixed output is obtained by joining together the upper end of the Rhythm, Fill, and Reverb potentiometers, and this is fed to the Left Hand Main amplifier from the output socket. The Pitch Control is connected via a non-reversible coupling to the Variable Frequency Oscillator. The function of this control is to vary the frequency of the VFO and thus the motor speed. The Volume control is intended as a means of setting the minimum volume of the instrument, that is the volume to which the output from the Right Hand Speaker falls when the Foot Pedal is fully closed. The coaxial sockets are of the insulated type to avoid interaction between the left hand and right hand earth system. The Foot Pedal is partly mechanical and partly electrical. If the panel volume control is set to zero resistance, the volume can be reduced to zero by the action of the foot pedal potentiometer. The Station Selection Switch is a six-button, self-canceling switch, which enables the direction and extent of cycling to be controlled by the player.

An Extension Speaker Panel is provided to enable the Mellotron to be used to operate loud-speakers other than those provided internally. As an additional facility, a coaxial line output socket is provided which may be used to drive external sound equipment, such as tape recorders or amplifiers.

CHAPTER 3

The Models

Mellotrons Come in Many Flavors

Mellotron Mark I

The Mark I was the earliest Mellotron, first built in 1963 with two 35-note keyboards side-by-side, and was based on the Chamberlin MusicMaster 600. It had the important addition of an internal subframe, which made a huge difference in mechanical reliability and eliminated problems associated with flexing of the cabinet. Chamberlin components were affixed directly to the cabinet. The Mark I also had improvements to the tape shuttling system. The Mark I was an elegant piece of cabinetry, with red mahogany veneer and a highly polished finish, not dissimilar to a decent upright piano as the instrument was originally a home instrument along the lines of an electronic organ. The first set of sounds reflected this as the very early Mark I units had no violins!

A light over each of the station selector switches came on to tell you that the Mellotron was ready to be played. They went off while you were changing banks, and if you tried to play them while in that mode, you almost certainly would have wrecked the tapes. At some stage before the Mark II was introduced, this problem was overcome by fitting a solenoid-controlled interlocking system that disabled the keys, so that you couldn't play even if you tried. Preamps were valve-type. The Bradleys had wanted to go solid-state, but the currently available designs were too noisy.

Mellotron Mark I # 132 (with Skellotron Owned by John Bradley)

The Mellotron Mark I was an advanced instrument for its time. As Mellotronics put it in its own brochure:

"The Mellotron is a revolutionary keyboard instrument providing pure music on triple channel pre-recorded tape. 18 different rhythms can be selected on the left-hand keyboard by means of a simply operated press button panel. On the right-hand keyboard, 18 different lead instruments are available on which you can play the melody of your

choice. The ingenious numbering system enables anyone with the slightest knowledge of music to play this fascinating instrument of the 60's."

***MEASUREMENTS:** 39" High x 51" Wide x 27" Deep.*
***WEIGHT:** 350 lbs.*
***VOLTAGES:** The instrument operates on all normal voltages.*
***AMPLIFICATION:** Transistorised amplifiers of special design are fitted together with full range volume controls.*
***LOUD SPEAKERS:** Two 12" heavy duty loudspeakers of high quality fitted. Output capacity 15 Watts each. Built in jacks for independent loudspeakers fitted as standard.*
***INSTRUCTION MANUAL:** A comprehensive instruction manual accompanies each instrument.*
***GUARANTEE:** Each instrument carries a 12 months guarantee.*
***SERVICING:** A service organisation is available.*

Practically all Mark I units were upgraded to Mark II specifications over the years, and probably most of them had already been done by 1965, as soon as they came back for service. The Meccano drive chain was the usual culprit, and was replaced with a Reynolds chain (as on Reynolds bicycles). John Bradley (Leslie's son) has an unmodified Mark I on which the Meccano chain works fine. The Mark I was very solid. It was definitely not designed for gigging, but was styled rather as a smart piece of mahogany furniture, weighing something like 140 kg (350 pounds), and had a rather posh "three-arse" matching bench seat with a back. The Mark I may have been monstrously heavy, but that didn't stop Bill Fransen, a massively strong man, from occasionally doing a party piece of lifting one bodily off the ground without assistance. Approximately 55 Mark I units were produced, mostly in 1963, with an original price of £1,000.

Mellotron Mark II

The so-called "king" of Mellotrons, the Mark II was a revised Mark I with minor transport and electronics improvements. It was the first totally successful Mellotron design, and was used on huge numbers of classic late '60s/early '70s tracks. See Appendix C for a rather exhaustive list of albums featuring the 'Tron.

Similarly to the Mark I and early Chamberlins, 3/8" tape was utilized, so a special tape-cutting machine had to be used. Although there has been debate as to why this format was chosen, Les Bradley says that it was simply because there wasn't enough room for half-inch mechanisms behind a standard keyboard. John Bradley says that you needed the wider tape to allow for the tolerances required by having heads that were mechanically shifted between the tracks. Others have stated that this was so people couldn't make their own tapes and would have to buy them at premium prices. It appears that the technical justification is sound because, with the benefit of hindsight and the lack of interest in the availability of a 1/4" conversion kit for the M400, it seems clear that the mass market was quite content with maintaining the status quo.

As with the Mark I, the Mark II was a complicated instrument to master. The left-hand keyboard played 17 different rhythms, ranging from a slow waltz to a raving rock sound (notes 1 through 17, with a coda on the lowest note) and 18 accompaniments (notes 18 through 35), while the right-hand keyboard played lead lines or chords, both using taped samples of instruments or ensembles, one for each note. Controls are mounted at an angle behind the keyboards. There are two six-position electrical station selector switches (one per keyboard) for shuttling between tape banks. Changing banks could take up to 20 seconds, as all

35 tapes had to be moved to new positions before playing could continue.

Photo Credit: Mellotron Archives

Mellotron Mark II # 123. Owned by David Kean.

There were also three mechanical track selector switches: the five-position switch on the right hand/ lead keyboard for track A, an A/B mix, track B, a B/C mix, and track C; the fill section on the left-hand keyboard has an identical five-position switch; and a five-position switch for the rhythms (no mix capability). There are separate volume controls for lead, rhythm, and fill sounds, plus a reverb control (lead sounds only), and a master pitch control. Besides the valve preamps, it housed two built-in 12″ speakers with solid-state power amps. The rhythm/fill tracks come out of the left side, the lead out of the right, but to increase spaciousness, the reverb on the lead came out of the left-hand side. The Mark II was disposed to the same problem as the early 400's, e.g., play too many notes at once (more than six or seven, on average) and the whole thing slowed down.

There was a one-off machine (projected name: Mini-Mellotron) that had just the left-hand rhythms and percussion tapes from the Mark II. The finish of most of the Mark II units was mahogany, but some were blond, one was white, and some were black with gold escutcheons. Approximately 250 Mark II units were built between 1964 and 1968, with an original price of £1,000.

Mellotron FX Console

The FX Console was a Mark II containing sound effects (1260 of them!) rather than instrument samples, with further electronic improvements. The BBC rightly saw the Mellotron as the best way to automate the sound effects (or more exactly, spot effects) for their productions. Their rigorous audio standards forced a lot of changes on the FX model as compared with the standard Mark II. Improvements in the capstan drive system, better signal-to-noise ratio due to separate head blocks and pre-amps, and electro-magnetic track selection (rather than mechanical) all contributed to a high quality machine. There was also no need for a big amplification system; rather, the FX had a small monitor amp and 8″ speaker.

The BBC bought several FX Consoles—painted black early on and later BBC regulation gray—and used them for any number of famous series, such as *Doctor Who*. These machines came up for auction a few years ago, and were knocked down very cheaply. Over the years, some of these machines have had music tapes refitted to them, giving an instrument that is sought after for recording. The Abbey Road Mellotron used on the Beatles' "White Album" was one of these. This same unit was bought at auction by Mike Oldfield for £1,000 in 1980, reacquired by Streetly Electronics, and subsequently purchased by Paul McCartney.

Mellotron FX Console

Other international broadcasting companies also took up the Mark II FX. Mellotronics must have reached some deal with the BBC over the copyright of the effects themselves (the masters of which had, of course, come from the BBC). Approximately 60 FX units were manufactured between 1965 and 1970, with an original price of £1,500.

The Mellotron 300

The Mellotron 300 is a single manual, 52-note model with six sound banks on two-track 1/4″ tape. As referenced before, maybe there was a point in using 3/8″ tape after all. This model, the only British Mellotron to use a different width of tape, was, to begin with, probably the least reliable of the lot. New recordings were made for the 300 that were different from the Mark II's sounds. From left to right on the keyboard, there are three notes of diminished chord riffs, an octave of backing tracks, three notes of percussion tracks, and then the rest are the lead sounds: 'melancholy' violins, flute, trombone, piano, vibes, clarinet, organ (in various drawbar settings), Spanish guitar, celeste, violin, and harpsichord. Recordings were generally of higher quality than on earlier models, mainly just from learning what worked and what didn't. The 300 also used a Hammond spring reverb, which Leslie Bradley admits was a good deal better than Bradmatics' own version (as used in Mark I and II units).

The 300 suffered some reliability problems, particularly relating to the tape guides, which had been re-designed. Their lubricant didn't last, causing static and problems when shuttling banks. As the self-lubricating properties of the Fluon tape guides failed, the result of changing banks was often broken tapes, as the 1/4″ tapes were more fragile than the 3/8″ tapes used on other models. (Wooly Wolstenholme of Barclay James Harvest got around this by never changing banks!) Martin Smith, though, says that it's quite possible (if not time-consuming) to replace the offending tape guides with rollers, and then the 300 should work well. Another downside was that after the first few units were produced, Mellotronics insisted on removing the pitch control and replacing the motor control and DC motor with a fixed speed AC motor. The reasoning behind this was that a "home keyboard" does not need to be tuned to anything else (a bit short-sighted really, imagine a Mellotron that can't be tuned!).

Mellotron 300

The Mellotron 300 was still fairly heavy, weighing in at about 100 kg. Approximately 60 units were produced between 1968 and 1970, with an original price of £1,500.

The Mellotron M400/400SM

The Mellotron M400 was introduced in 1970. This model was a single manual (G-F) 35-note Mellotron with one sound bank on three-track 3/8" tape, mounted on a removable tape frame "cassette." This was far simpler and thus more reliable than the 300. There was only one bank on each tape frame, so no problems fast-forwarding or rewinding to another bank, which was the source of most of the problems with the 300. The 400 also made up for the comparative paucity of sounds by making it infinitely easier to swap tape frames. There was a good range of tapes available, much more so than the Mark II: violins (from solo to full orchestra section), viola, cello, flute, clarinet, oboe, bassoon, brass, trombone, French horn, tenor sax, trombone/trumpet section, tenor/alto sax section, church organ, honky tonk piano, Clavinet, Rhodes, vibes, marimba, Minimoog, VCS3, electric and acoustic guitars, mandolin, small and large choirs, loads of percussion and sound effects, 48 in all. Tape racks came in suitcases that were a bit like cymbal cases.

The standard three sounds were most usually flute, 3 violins, and cello, but a lot of other permutations were also recommended, such as church organ and choirs, violin/viola/cello, and so on. You could also supply sounds on 1/4" tape for Mellotronics to turn into Mellotron tapes. There was also the option to buy a set of 1/4" tape guides, which would enable you to use your own standard 1/4" tapes in the Mellotron. You could not, of course, use the original 3/8" tapes anymore unless you swapped the tape guides back. Also, while in the 1/4" format, you would be limited to two tracks instead of three.

Photo Credit: Mike Grueterich

Mellotron M400 with tape frame and case

The 400 had very simple controls, mounted to the left of the keyboard: level (volume), range (passive tone control), and varispeed (pitch), plus a three-position switch for selecting which of the three sounds you wanted. The 400 was almost portable compared with other Mellotrons. There was no built-in amp and speaker, and it used transistors (rather than valves), so it was much, much lighter (although still not a one-person job to shift, by any means).

Early models had the potentially problematic CMC10 motor drive system, which would exhibit the old problem of slowing down if more than six or seven notes were played at once, with disastrous results for pitch. It could also put out a high-pitched whine, which could even break through into the audio output. Later models (from 1973/4 on, it was the 400SM) had the SMS2 motor systems, which were far superior.

Photo Credit: Mellotron Archives

Clear Perspex Mellotron 400SM

There was one clear perspex model built, presumably for promotional purposes, which is now owned by Mellotron Archives. One left-handed model was built for Paul McCartney, with the controls on the right-hand side of the keyboard. Tape frames were expensive (£195 each), but they had to be made to very fine tolerances, and then looked after to stop them from going out of true. A "Mellotron Mixer" was an optional extra, with extra 3-band EQ and volume control. There were three line/mic inputs so that you could put vocals in with your Mellotron through your combo amp (big live mixing desks weren't very common in those days). The mixers were made by another manufacturer to Bradmatics' specifications. Probably only about 12 were made. And no Mellotron would be complete without its Protector Muff, an amazing padded carrying case with great big bondage straps, and a padded pouch for the volume pedal and mains lead.

There were about 2,000 Mellotron/Novatron units manufactured between 1970 and 1986, not including a batch of about 100 teak-flavored machines that were made under license by EMI, which all have an E4 prefix to their serial number. The original selling price was £795.

The Mellotron 400 FX

This model was a Mellotron 400 specifically designed for sound effects work. There were 105 instant spot effects on each tape frame, with a library of 1260 sounds effects available. The tone control was replaced by a 'monitor' control that determined the volume of the signal coming out of the additional headphone socket on the front. This allowed the operator to determine what the next sound effect cue sounded like while the main volume was down which was more useful than the original tone control as EQ and effects would be added externally. The manufacturers claimed a tape frame change time of two minutes for this or the ordinary 400. About ten 400 FX's were made between 1970 and 1984, although another 20 or so standard M400's were converted and sold as FX machines to various broadcasting companies around the world. The original price was £2,100 with all 12 tape frames.

Photo Credit: Mike Grueterich

Mellotron EMI M400

The Mellotron Mark V

This is a dual manual Mellotron, essentially a double Mellotron 400. The keyboard layout is similar to the Mark II, but the controls were re-positioned in front of the keyboards. A stereo headphone socket was provided, and there were two volume pedals sticking out from underneath. Left and right outputs were provided, and you could pan each keyboard's output between them. The controls were really just like two sets of Mellotron 400 controls, with the addition of reverb. Frank Bradley, a very thorough and logical man, was heavily involved in the design work.

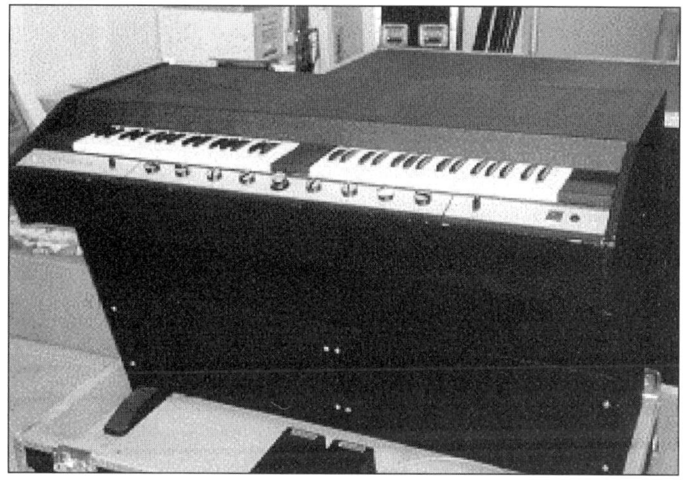

Photo Credit: Mark Clinsk

Mellotron Mark V

The new casing gave the Mark V a bold, thrusting look for the mid-seventies, with the bottom panel sloping back away from you to give an impression that the keyboard is stretching out towards the player. During Novatron production, Streetly finally ran out of the steel castings used on all of the small flywheel models M400/MKV/T550 and decided to machine subsequent flywheels out of solid steel. The greater mass of these contributed to the stability of the machine, and, of course, the weight). All were finished in black Tolex. The only white one in the world was painted white by Edgar Froese of Tangerine Dream. The Mark V is quite possibly the most desirable of all Mellotrons, for its rarity, and for the way it combines the huge power of the Mark II with the flexibility and good sounds of the 400, including choir sounds in a dual manual Mellotron for the first time.

The Mark V was not a great commercial success. According to John Bradley, there were 31 units made (including the prototype, built in 1974) between 2/13/75 and 2/7/80 before the demise of Mellotronics, the last four of which were labeled Novatrons. The original price was £2,200 with your choice of two tape frames and "Cripple Creek" hard-shell case.

The Novatron 400SM

This model was virtually identical to the Mellotron 400. This, again, was the name the Bradley brothers adopted for the instrument after losing the rights to the Mellotron name in the aftermath of the DMI debacle. Most of the units were white, as the Mellotron 400, but a black-finished version was also available, and towards the end of the run became the norm. You could choose your own tape set. One typical set was brass, strings, and flute.

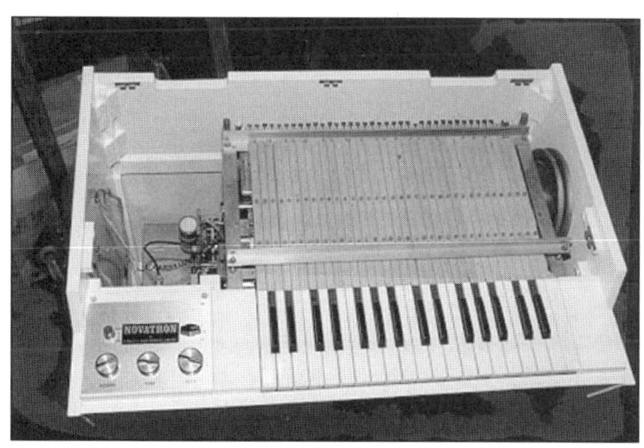

Photo Credit: Streetly Electronics

Novatron 400SM

A noise gate became available as an optional extra in 1980 in response to the fact that the Novatron's competitors, the samplers, were staring to sound much, much better than the original Fairlights and Emulators. As with most Mellotrons, the signal was pretty hot, and could cause distortion if you didn't attenuate it. It would have made good marketing sense for Streetly to have installed a switchable attenuator in the output circuit. What they did instead was sell a Mellotron Attenuator box as an optional extra. The original selling price of the Novatron 400SM was £1,374.

Photo Credit: Mellotron Archives

Novatron T550

The Novatron Mark V

As with the Mellotron/Novatron 400, this model was identical to the Mellotron Mark V. When the Bradley Brothers were forced to adopt the Novatron name, they took out advertisements telling clients that they would continue making exactly the same model range—the 400SM and the Mark V. Only four Novatron Mark V units were made. The original selling price was £2,200 with two tape frames of your choice.

The Novatron T550

This is a flight case version of the Mellotron/Novatron 400SM, the brainchild of Frank Bradley. The T550 is practically identical to the 400SM, and was a heavy but roadworthy Mellotron designed to appeal to that dwindling number of bands for whom only the original real thing would do. It had a hinged keyboard lid, removable front panel with space for two tape frames and the swell pedal in transit. There was also a hinged rear door for 'service accessibility'. There were probably only three made (c. 1982)—a sad indication of Mellotron's decline in the market. At this writing, Streetly Electronics will be manufacturing a limited number of new T-550 units. The original selling price was £999.

The Mellotron 4-Track

This was the direction taken by Sound Sales, the American firm headed by Bill Eberline, who had handled Mellotron's servicing and spare parts business in the United States, and who, thanks to a bureaucrat's blunder, ended up buying the inventory and the right to use the Mellotron name when Mellotronics went into receivership. The 4-Track used quarter-inch tape, was externally similar to a Mellotron 400, and used basically the same tape rack design. The casing, however, was sheet aluminum, and had a bit of a washing machine look. It was available in black, white, or blue.

Rationalizing to this size of tape (1/4") and number of tracks does seem like a good idea—if the thinner width of tape didn't make too many demands on the accuracy of the transport system and gentleness of tape-handling. Using a fixed tape head block rather than moving ones as on the Chamberlin and British Mellotrons, of course, made the tolerances much less critical.

The Mellotron 4-Track had seven outputs: left, right, mono, and one each for the four preamps. The control panel was placed to the left of the keyboard, as in the 400, and included an on/off switch, volume, three-band EQ for each track, and a master pitch control. This coupled with the ability to punch in any of the four tracks, made it a flexible live and recording instrument, if the quality of the original factory tapes, which were poorly produced, had been high enough. Mellotron Archives has produced new tapes that showcase the 4-Track in a much better light.

There are mixed opinions on the relative success of this as a Mellotron. It should be emphasized that this model has no connection whatsoever to the Bradley Brothers, and was strictly a Sound Sales venture. There were only 4 units produced, with an original selling price of $4,500.

Photo Credit: Robert Laughton

Mellotron 4-Track #02. Owned by Robert Laughton.

The Digital Mellotron

The Digital Mellotron, only existing as a prototype and never having been seen outside of captivity, recently surfaced (in November 1999) and was put up for auction on eBay.com. As described online, "the Studio Symphony by Mellotron is a true 16-bit, 24-voice polyphonic sample playback system. This system has been designed with the recording studio in mind. The design philosophy behind the audio circuitry in their product has been 'cost is no object' purity. All audio components are of the finest quality.

"In addition to .004% THD and 96db of dynamic range, the audio path maintains less than 10 degrees of phase error at 20kHz for true stereo recording and playback. The audio outputs are pro level (+4dbv) and have plenty of current capability for driving long runs of low impedance lines. Leading edge data conversion technology allows for recording at sample rates of 48kHz or 96kHz. Playback sample rates can be as high as 192kHz. The unit includes 24 voices, 4 Meg of battery backed up RAM, and a SCSI interface to facilitate soundfile transfers and control functions by way of an IBM PC or compatible. The sample memory can be expanded to 32 Megs in 4 Meg increments and is partitioned into 4 segments—each one fourth of the total installed RAM. The control processor in the Studio Symphony can be playing samples back from all RAM segments, or it can take control of one of the RAM segments to load new sounds while simultaneously playing sounds from the other three segments.

"The unit features two MIDI inputs and can accept MIDI data from both simultaneously. It can also be configured as two or more completely separate instruments with fixed or dynamic voice allocation. Full multi-timbral MIDI implementation is supported including velocity sensitive crossfades and layering. The Studio Symphony not only initiates sample playback via MIDI control, but will accept 5 volt trigger inputs for each voice with only a few microseconds of time delay before audio is output. This feature is invaluable for automatic track replacement. Microtonal tuning capability allows pitch accuracy of better than 1 cent and the creation of user defined keyboard temperaments. The Studio Symphony responds to MIDI pitch bend and modulation inputs and will pitch bend up one octave and down two octaves. In addition to velocity sensitive amplitude, the attack and decay time of the samples can be adjusted, or an envelope function table can be applied to the sample for high resolution amplitude shaping. The Studio Symphony comes with stereo (L, R) and mono (L+R) outputs at a nominal output level of +4dbv."

The opening bid for this unit was $50,000. There were no takers.

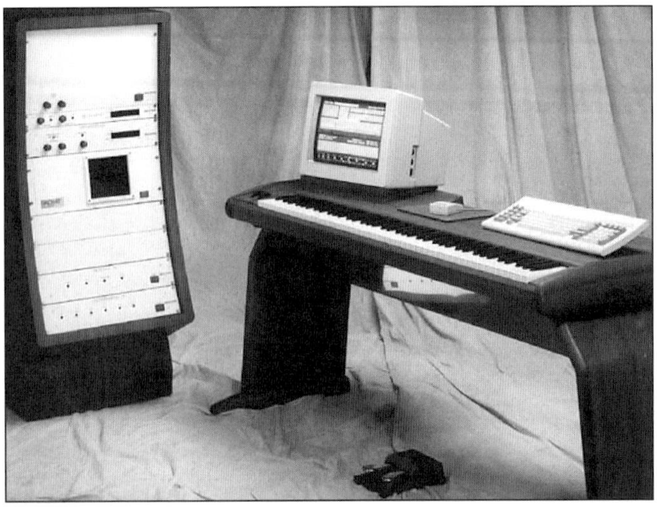

Photo Credit: unknown

Digital Mellotron–Studio Symphony

The Mellotron Mark VI

The Mellotron Mark VI is the newest generation of Mellotrons, manufactured and distributed by Mellotron Archives in North Hollywood, California. The exterior of the Mellotron Mark VI looks like a Mellotron 400. A white cabinet is standard, but other finish options and reversed key colors are available. The functions and features of the old Mellotron 400 are preserved in the new model. The keyboard has wooden keys in the same way as the old Mellotrons, and the tape frames are interchangeable.

According to Mellotron Archives, Mellotron Mark VI units contain the following enhancements to the classic Mellotron we all know and love:

Tube preamp: *A specially developed tube preamp similar to the Mark II giving improved sonic qualities, i.e., signal-to-noise ratio of 65/70 dbm, as opposed to 55 dbm.*

Baltic Birch cabinet: *The cabinets are made of high quality birch plywood. With corner reinforcements and a thicker bottom plate, the cabinets are both stronger and much lighter than any of the original cabinets.*

Stainless Steel Capstan: *The Mellotron Mark VI features a stainless steel precision polished capstan. This capstan will never rust or pit and since it is extremely hard it will not wear. This assembly matched with a slightly heavier flywheel affords more inertial mass and therefore, even more stability.*

Metric Hardware: *Standard metric hardware. Ever try to find British Association thread fasteners outside of Britain?*

Taller Cabinet: *The original Rosewood and Oak Mellotron 400 cabinet dimensions are used. In short, the cabinet is 2" taller for increased playability while still maintaining the classic, instantly recognizable shape of a Mellotron from all angles.*

Two Speed Motor Control: *A dual pitch stability improved motor control system. At the flick of a switch change the pitch of the sounds to a different user-preset value.*

New Stable Motor: *The new motor is a high stability precision motor that is much better suited for constant-speed applications than the old motor. Because of the improved torque of this motor, the ratio between the pulley and flywheel could be changed to allow the motor to run at optimum rpm and add a slight increase in flywheel diameter. The increased mass to the flywheel results in a greater stabilizing effect on the capstan, resulting in both higher playing stability and better pitch change response (for achieving the Mark II "slide-effect").*

Non-Warping Keyboard: *The basswood keys on many original Mellotrons 400's have warped. A collaboration with Herrburger, Brooks Ltd (the original manufacturer) solved this problem with a kiln dried pine that is treated to resist warping and twisting.*

New Tape Frame Design: *The new style tape frame is already in use in dozens of Mellotron 400's and is lighter and more robust than the old frame. It also supports longer tapes, increasing the playing time per note by approximately 20%.*

Tuning Indicator: *An indicator on the control panel shows when the flywheel is running at the desired speed.*

Balanced Outputs: *A true professional-quality balanced audio output is included in addition to a standard TS unbalanced line output.*

High Quality Pots: *The audio pots, pitch pot and the trim pots are of the highest quality.*

Remastered Sounds: *The Mellotron and Chamberlin sounds have been remastered from the original session tapes, giving much better sonic clarity and higher reproduction quality. Some sounds (like the Mellotron Glockenspiel) have never been available before. In addition, new sounds have been added (like Recorder and 35-note Female Voice) and the entire Chamberlin library is available to Mellotron owners.*

Improved Keyboard Action: *Touch sensitivity on a Mellotron! People who have played a meticulously adjusted Mellotron know that you can get a different attack to the sound depending on how fast you press the key down. The new keyboard makes it much easier to achieve this effect and provides for a much more dynamic sounding instrument.*

Lighter Overall Weight: *Predominantly because of its modern, much lighter power supply, improved frame design and a Baltic birch plywood cabinet, the total weight of the Mark VI is less than that of a standard 400 — despite the fact that the Mark VI is slightly taller.*

The initial run of Mark VI Mellotrons, in early 1999, was 30 units: 20 for sale in the United States and 10 available in Europe and the United Kingdom. There was a second run in November 1999. This production also meant that many new parts also could be used as spare parts for old Mellotrons, making it possible to "resurrect" even more of the original machines. Mark VI's are available for $5,200, which includes an ATA-rated flight case on locking rollers, plus shipping.

Photo Credit: Mellotron Archives

Mellotron Mark VI

CHAPTER 4

The Pictures

Photo Credit: Martin Smith

Mellotron Mark I #103 upgraded to Mark II specifications
Owned by John McClain

Photo Credit: Jerry Korb

Mellotron Mark I #124 with JK-MK VI prototype
Owned by Jerry Korb

Photo Credit: Streetly Electronics

Mellotron Mark I #124. Owned by Jerry Korb.

Photo Credit: Jerry Korb

Jerry Korb (left) and John Bradley with JK-MK VI prototype designed and built by Jerry Korb.

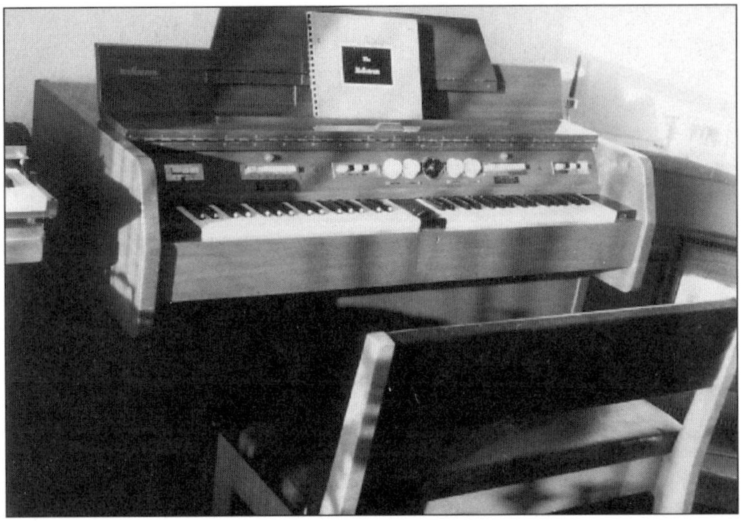

Photo Credit: John Bradley

Mellotron Mark I #132 (unmodified) with "three-arse bench." Owned by John Bradley.

Photo Credit: Robert Young

Mellotron Mark II #118. Owned by Robert Young.

Photo Credit: Frank Samagaio

Mellotron Mark II #123. Owned by David Kean.

Photo Credit: Frank Samagaio

Mellotron Mark II #23. Owned by David Kean.

Photo Credit: David Cilia

Mellotron Mark II #220 (in polished black finish). Owned by Alain Celos.

Photo Credit: David Cilia

Mellotron Mark II #220 (in polished black finish). Owned by Alain Celos.

Photo Credit: Robert Cervero

"In fhe Court of the Crimson King" Mellotron Mark II #113. Owned by Robert Fripp.

Photo Credit: Robert Cervero

"In the Wake of Poseidon" Mellotron Mark II #232. Owned by Robert Fripp.

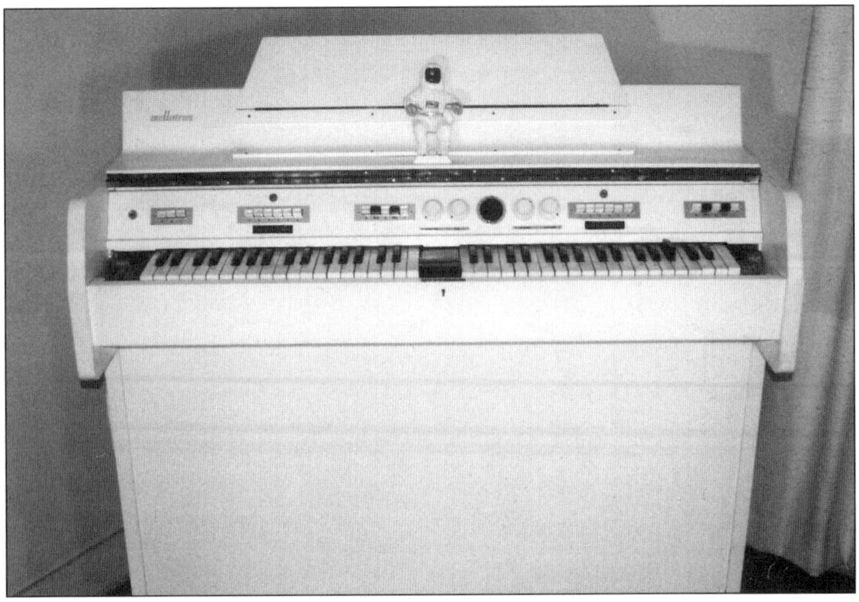

Photo Credit: Brian Kehew

Mellotron Mark II #125. Owned by Brian Kehew.

Photo Credit: Frank Samagaio

Mellotron Mark II #238. Owned by Justin Mayer.

Photo Credit: Ken Merbler

Mellotron Mark II #247. Owned by Ken Merbler.

Photo Credit: Ken Leonard

Mellotron Mark II SFX Console #10030. Owned by Rick Blechta.

Photo Credit: Damon Fox

Mellotron Mark II Music Console. Owned by Damon Fox of Bigelf, formerly owned by Martin Kitkat of Gracious.

Photo Credit: Pierre Veilleux

The Pierre Veilleux Mellotron Constellation M400's #709 & 745 (front), Mark II #258 (left), M300 #046 (rear), and Mark V #128 (right).

Photo Credit: David Cilia

Mellotron 300 #003. Owned by David Cilia.

Photo Credit: David Cilia

Mellotron 300 #003. Owned by David Cilia.

Photo Credit: Jerry Korb

Mellotron 300 #037. Owned by Jerry Korb.

Photo Credit: Jerry Korb

Mellotron 300 #037. Owned by Jerry Korb.

Photo Credit: Robert Cervero

Mellotron M400 #354 "Islands" 'Tron. Owned by Robert Fripp.

Photo Credit: Norm Leete

Mellotron M400 #V1514. Owned by Norm Leete, formerly owned by Wooly Wolstenholme/Barclay James Harvest.

Photo Credit: David Cilia

Mellotron 400SM #1671. Owned by David Cilia.

Photo Credit: David Cilia

Mellotron 400SM #1671. Owned by David Cilia.

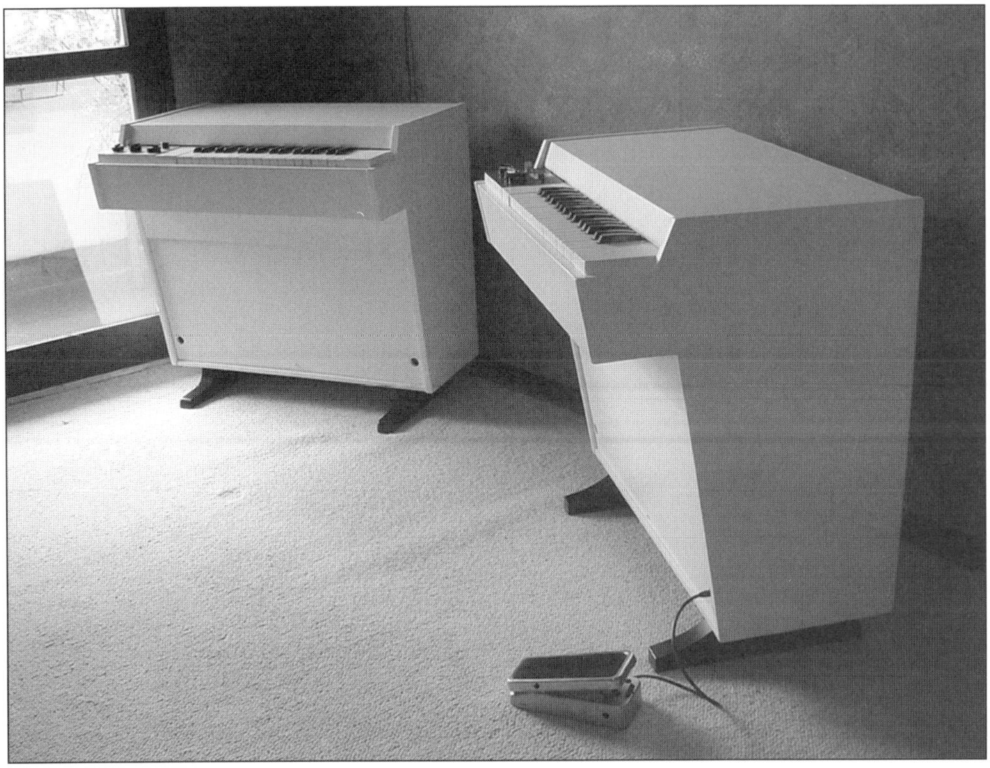

Photo Credit: David Cilia

Mellotron 400SM #256. Owned by David Cilia.

Photo Credit: Frank Samagaio

Solid Oak Mellotron 400SM. Owned by David Kean.

Photo Credit: Adam Scramstad

Mellotron M400 #908, refinished in walnut stain.
Owned by Frank Samagaio.

Photo Credit: David Shapiro

EMI Mellotron M400 #E4/169S. Owned by David Shapiro.

Photo Credit: Norm Leete

EMI Mellotron M400–the "Frankentron" before restoration by Streetly Electronics. Formerly owned by Norm Leete; present owner unknown.

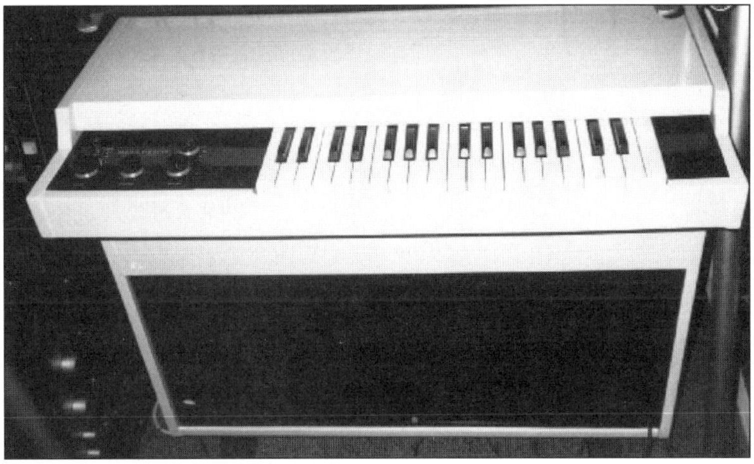

Photo Credit: Norm Leete

EMI Mellotron M400–the "Frankentron" after restoration by Streetly Electronics. Formerly owned by Norm Leete; present owner unknown.

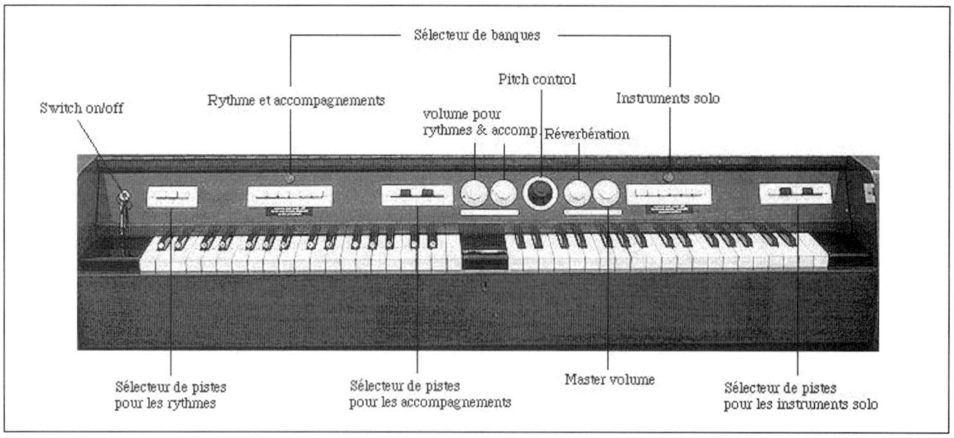

Photo Credit: Mellotron Archives

Mellotron Mark I/II Control Panel

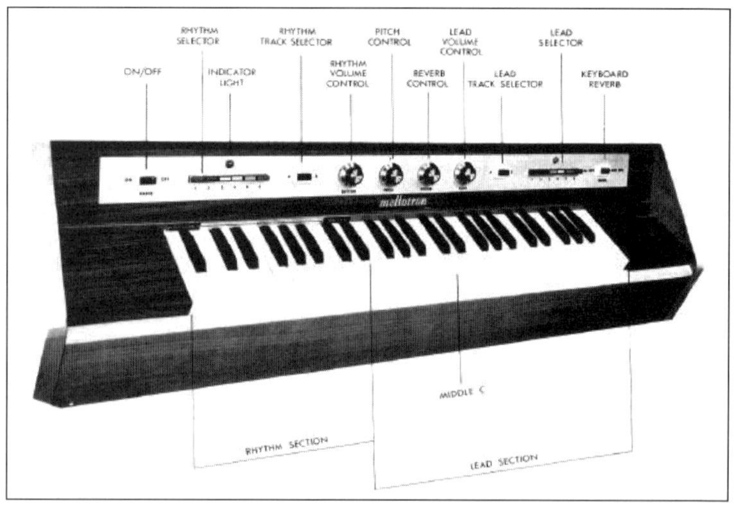

Photo Credit: Mellotron Archives

Mellotron 300 Control Panel

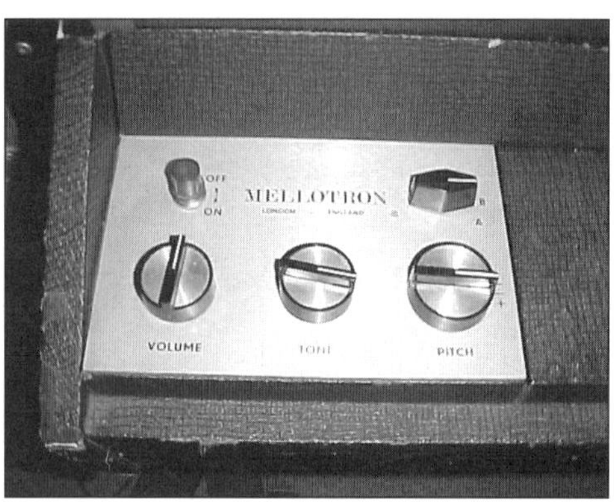

Photo Credit: Mellotron Archives

M400/400SM Control Panels

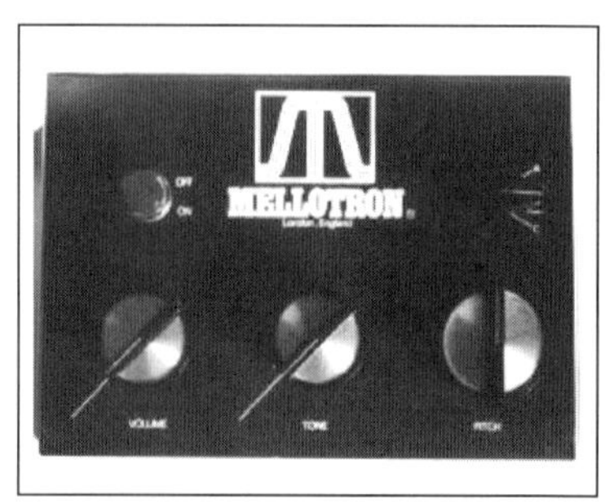

Photo Credit: Mellotron Archives

M400/400SM Control Panels

Photo Credit: Mellotron Archives

Mellotron Mark VI Control Panel

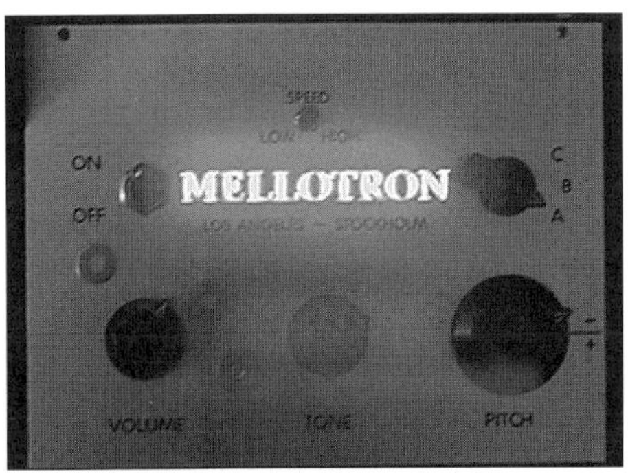

Photo Credit: Mellotron Archives

Mellotron Mark VI Control Panel

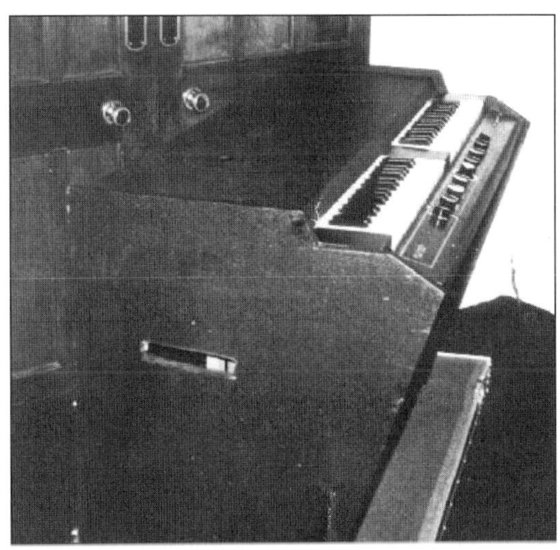

Photo Credit: unknown

Mellotron Mark V. Owned by Jimmy Page.

Photo Credit: Pierre Veilleux

Mellotron Mark V #128. Owned by Pierre Veilleux.

Photo Credit: Mellotron Archives

Novatron T550. Streetly Electronics will soon make a limited number of these units available.

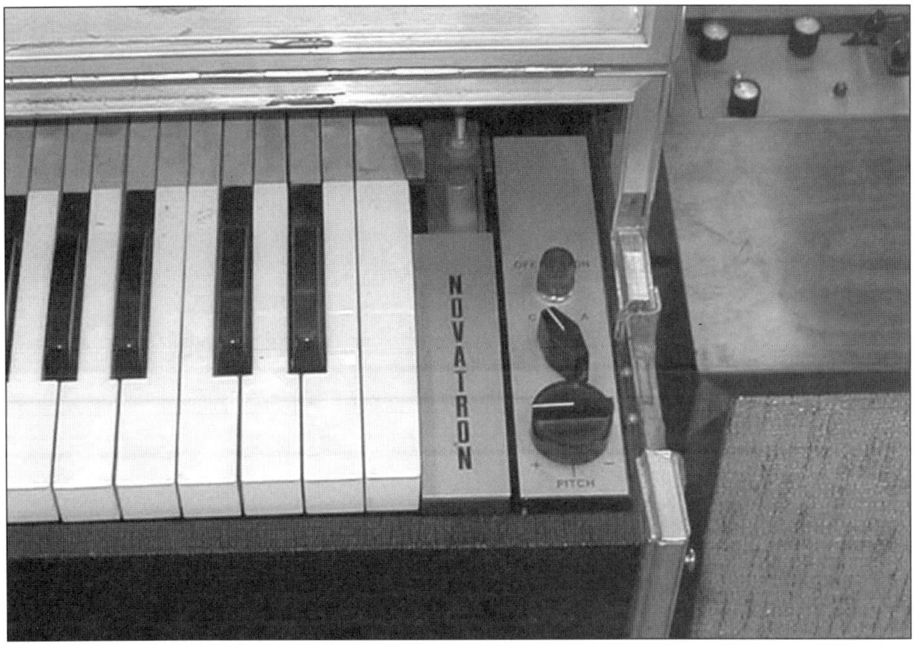

Photo Credit: Mellotron Archives

Novatron T550

Photo Credit: Mellotron Archives

Novatron T550

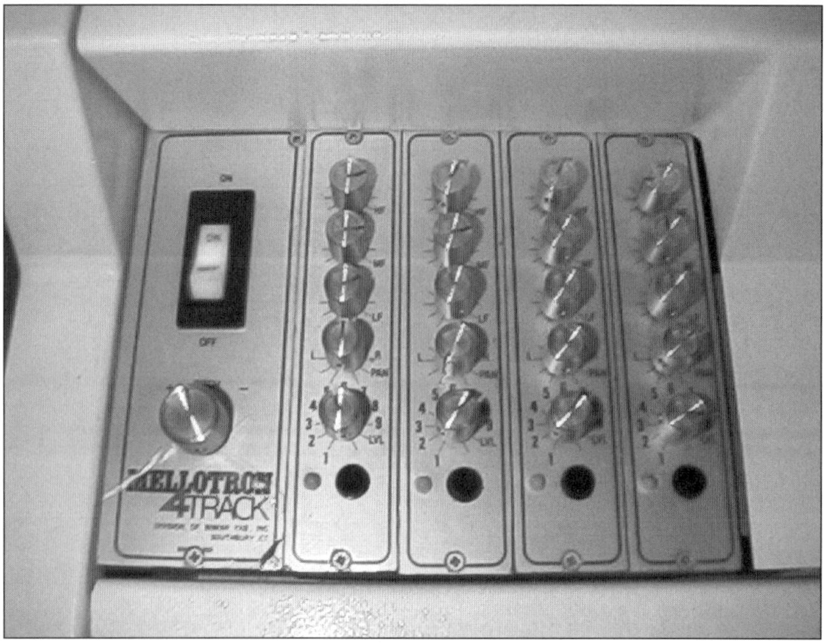

Photo Credit: Robert Laughton

Mellotron 4-Track control panel. Owned by Robert Laughton.

Photo Credit: Robert Laughton

Mellotron 4-Track #02. Owned by Robert Laughton.

Photo Credit: Mellotron Archives

Mellotron Mark VI #008 after assembly at Mellotron Archives.
Owned by Noel Gallagher.

Photo Credit: Mellotron Archives

An early version of the Mellotron.

Photo Credit: Rick Blechta

Snovatron #001. For that classic "icy" Mellotron sound.

Photo Credit: Mellotron Archives

Les Bradley at the keyboard of the Mark II, with an M300 in the background and a 400 immediately behind him.

Photo Credit: Mellotron Archives

Harry Chamberlin seated at the Riviera.

Photo Credit: Mellotron Archives

Chamberlin Music Master 600. This unit is similar to the ones Bill Fransen presented to the Bradley Brothers in 1962, and cosmetically akin to its eventual offspring, the Mellotron Mark I/II. Approximately 100 units were produced between 1962-1969.

Photo Credit: Mellotron Archives

Chamberlin MusicMaster 200. Owned by Zac Rae. Approximately 200 units were produced between 1951-1959.

Photo Credit: Mellotron Archives

Chamberlin Riviera. Owned by David Kean. This was Harry Chamberlin's personal instrument. It uses 8-track tape, has stereo outputs, and consists of 5 independent M-1-style units. Only 2 were made in 1970.

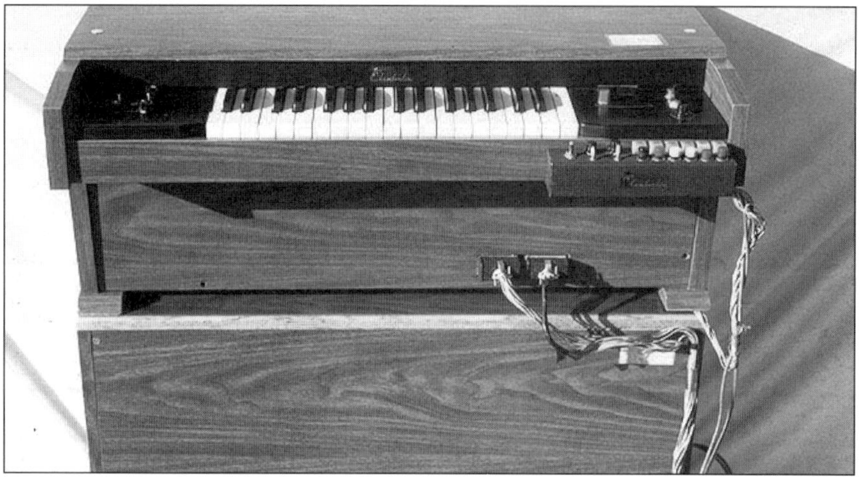

Photo Credit: Mellotron Archives

Chamberlin M1 w/ M1 Remote. Harry Chamberlin's finest effort. Uses 8-track tape, stereo heads, 52-note range. Approximately 100 units were produced between 1970-1981. Owned by David Kean.

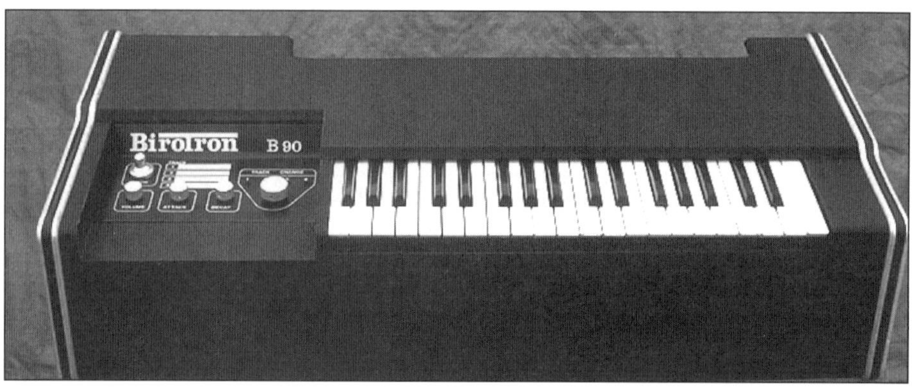

Photo Credit: Mellotron Archives

Birotron B90 #007. The Birotron was the collaborative brainchild of Rick Wakeman and Dave Biro. Tapes were on 8-track cartridges in a continous loop.

Photo Credit: Mellotron Archives

Vako Orchestron. Owner unknown. Developed by Dave VanKoevering, using laser-read optical disks.

Photo Credit: Justin Mayer

J-Tron #001. Designed and owned by Justin Mayer. Originally built in 1993-94, the J-Tron was designed and built by Justin Mayer with an eye towards combining and improving upon the features of both Chamberlins and Mellotrons that he felt were most successful. Its current version includes stereo heads, 2 stations of 8-track tape with manual shuttle, simpler track selector, and a new library of sounds.

Photo Credit: Justin Mayer

J-Tron #001

SAMWIT

The first Semi-Annual Mellotron Workshop In Toronto (SAMWIT) was held on May 20-21, 2000 in Toronto, Ontario, Canada. It was conducted by John Bradley and Martin Smith of Streetly Electronics. Mellotron owners and enthusiasts were able to come together for the very first time, spending the weekend in hands-on activities, maintenance, and repair of various Mellotrons, along with abundant mirth and merriment. Thanks to Rick Blechta and Chris Dale for organizing the event, and to Craig Collett of Coll Audio for the use of his facility.

SAMWIT Photo Credits: Ken Leonard, Ken Merbler, Jim Kreuger p54-59

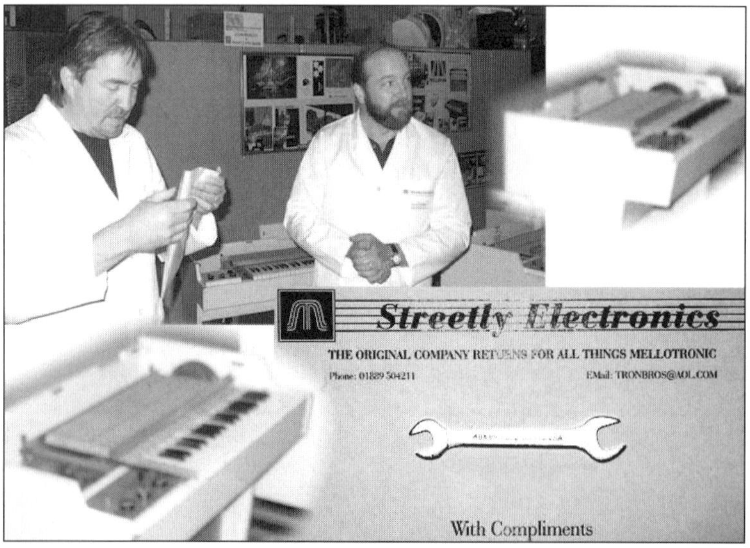

Martin Smith (Mellotron Brother #2) and John Bradley (Mellotron Brother #1)

John and Martin presenting the first new production tape frame #001 to John McIntyre.

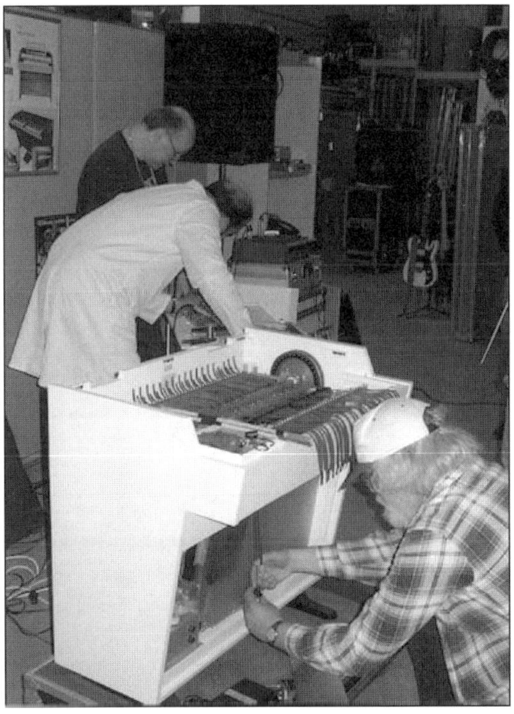

John McIntyre installing new tapes on his new tape frame.

A rear inner view of Rick Blechta's SFX Console

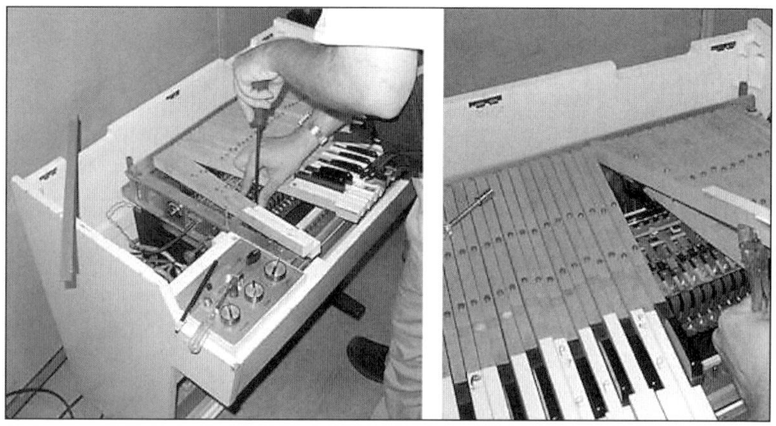

Ken Leonard adjusting the keyboard of M400 #805.

Pierre Veilleux and Frank Samagaio making adjustments to the SFX keyboard.

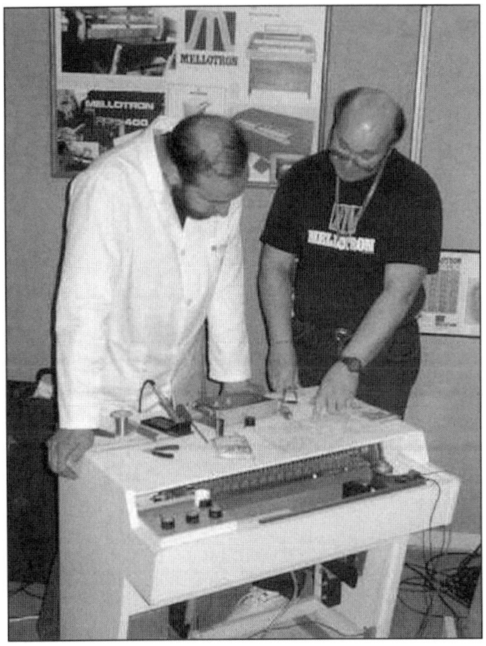

John B. and Jerry Korb troubleshooting a problem.

Rick Blechta's SFX Console #10030

John B. showing Joe Ferrainola how to change a tape frame.

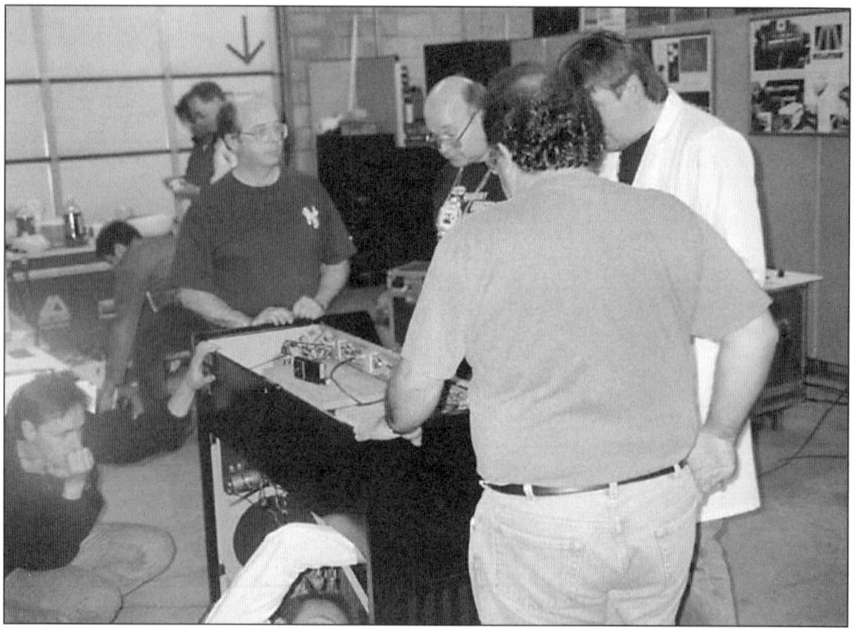

Working on the SFX Console

Cleaning the SFX pinch rollers

Behind Rick B.'s SFX Console: Joe Ferrainola, "Professor" Jerry Korb, Jimmy Moore, Frank Samagaio, John Bradley, Rick Blechta, Martin Smith, Chris Dale ("Hey, everybody! It's Chris Dale!"), Ken Leonard, Ken Merbler (standing); Fritz "Puff" Doddy, Craig Collett, Pierre Veilleux (kneeling).

CHAPTER 5

The Experience

Famous and Behind-the-Scenes Owners and Users of the Mellotron Share Their Personal Experiences.

Some of the most enlightening methods, tips, tricks, and anecdotes about the Mellotron come straight from the people who have used the 'Tron over the past four decades. To that end, the author interviewed numerous Mellotron users in an attempt to showcase both the varied techniques and strong feelings that this instrument elicits.

Some of the general questions the author asked the interviewees for this section were:

When did you first hear and/or become aware of the Mellotron, and how did it strike you at the time?

Did you have that same "aha" revelation that many Mellotron enthusiasts reported experiencing?

How do the limitations of the instrument affect your playing approach (i.e., eight-second playability, tape transport reliability, etc.)?

What techniques do you use in recording the Mellotron (i.e., use of EQ, reverb, effects, etc.)?

Which models have you owned/used?

Are there any Mellotron war stories/anecdotes/oddities from gigs (your own or those you've witnessed) that strike you as worth telling (i.e., times when performing with a Mellotron went either spectacularly well or spectacularly badly)?

Mike Pinder (Moody Blues, solo artist; contributor of "Waters Beneath the Bridge" to *The Rime of the Ancient Sampler–The Mellotron Album* CD)

Mike Pinder

On the experience of working at Streetly Electronics:

It was the first time that the sound in that form had been used. I had no idea what the Mellotron was at the time. The ad (in the *Birmingham Mail*) read, "Wanted–person with musical and electronic knowledge–please apply." Those were the two things that I had a modicum of. My dad, Burt, was into electronics, made crystal sets, repaired radios, and tinkered with stuff, so the smell of solder was as distinctive to me as an apple pie on Aunt Jemima's kitchen window, if you know what I mean. There was the electronic experience there. I had an insight in, and understood the basic circuitry and principles, like why the pre-amplifier came before the amplifier and not after it. I felt I had enough going, and lo and behold, that was it. I'm there, they showed me around, and showed me the machine to start off with. It was that moment of bliss, in a sense, that I realized it was what I was looking for, having no idea that something like this had already been invented.

I'd never come across any literature about it. For me, part of the revelation was that here I was, putting my hands on the keyboard of an instrument that allowed me to get very close, in a sense, to things I was hearing in my head. And that right there was quite an incredible thing, because the people who had had that kind of privilege were people like Beethoven, Bach and other great guys who could hear everything and were able to write it down and, hence, what we have now. I think that in a small way, someone who didn't have that kind of musical background or talent could still express themselves musically, albeit a limited expression compared with a real orchestra. The whole idea of being able to make orchestrations with real instrument sounds was absolutely fantastic to me.

I didn't have the band then, when I discovered the Mellotron. We just finished a band, actually. Ray Thomas and I had put a very quick band together to go to Germany and do some things in Hamburg and the Top Ten Club. We were right on the heels of the Beatles. We did a few months over there, and when we got back, Ray went back to work at a tool making company. I didn't have a regular job to go back to, was looking for something to do, read the paper, and found the "ad of destiny" for me. This was 1963. I formed the band, the original Moody Blues 5, on March 15th, 1964. I left Streetly Electronics deliberately to form the band, a new band, which was to include Ray. The first thing I did was to give my notice at Streetly Electronics and that afternoon, I got in my car and drove down to Ray's factory. He was outside eating a sandwich sitting on a wall. I came up to him and said, "Ray, go give your notice, it's time to start the new band." And that's how it all started. I wasn't able to buy a Mellotron, it was just too expensive, and I'd never seen that kind of money. They were something like 3,000 pounds

But the overall ecstasy was sort of almost like an undreamt dream coming about. The whole idea of actually being able to portray orchestral sounds in the band was just something that I knew I had to do. Getting the money was not going to be that easy, but I just went ahead regardless, knowing that I needed to get one of these machines. The only way I could get one was to earn more money than I was making being the quality control guy at Streetly. It was inevitable that I had to leave to go out and put a band together that would be worthy enough to make the project work. From the very beginning when Ray and I went out for the first time to find a bass player, a drummer, and a singer, it was always, "And I've got this machine, I don't have one yet, but there is this machine that we have to get."

It was never possible in the first band (the "Go Now" Moody Blues) because we were signed to a management company and they were in between all the contracts that we had, agency and recording-wise, which meant all the money went to them and then they paid us an allowance, which was really just enough to have a reasonable flat, a used set of wheels, and to buy reasonable instruments. But there were no surplus monies at that time. Our best times were nearly always while we were touring because we got extra expenses. That's how it was when we first started, the "Go Now" days, especially. We ended the "Go Now" days absolutely broke because the management company closed up shop and disappeared, never to be seen again, with all the money from "Go Now." We were cheated out of our royalties. Also, the main delay (in getting the Mellotron), why I didn't actually end up getting one when we were successful, was because of the money.

Les Bradley (of Streetly Electronics) gave me a call, and because we had talked about it beforehand, said that perhaps someone would have a used one. He did call me one day and said, "You know, Mike, I found a Mellotron machine and it's down at the Dunlop Social Club, the Dunlop Tyre Company. So I went off to see it, and that was it. Three hundred pounds; it was a steal. The Bradley Brothers were all just wonderful. I'm really proud to have known them and worked for them. They were kind, generous, and thoughtful. It was great. Best regular job I ever had."

On using the Mellotron on early recordings and performances:

There were no DC motors available; it was AC. That was why when we got to a gig if Mrs. Smith, Mrs. Jones, and Mrs. Edwards down the road had just put on their electric ovens to cook their husbands' dinner, the voltage would go down, the amperage would go down on the line, and so would the pitch on the Mellotron. The speed of the motor would slow down and I'd be out of tune. A lot of times I had to actually be tuning with my left hand while I was playing things on the right, which is why I ended up having strong single, and occasional two or three note lines. I had to structure my playing around the limitations of the instrument itself, taking into account my own limitations as a musician, and that's what I ended up with. That was my deliberate approach to playing it, to try to make it as simple as possible, make it strong and not to clutter it too much, to try and create some distance. One of my favorite intervals is tenths, having a lot of space between what's happening as opposed to close hand for fingerfuls or handfuls of notes. It generally doesn't work very well on strings, but under certain circumstances it does. For the most part, nice linear lines would seem to work best.

On the modifications to his Mark II:

It actually came with a VFO, the AC version, which was fairly simple, but then I got wind of printed circuit DC motors being manufactured. Eventually, I think that they came just a little bit afterwards, but I did put printed circuit DC motors in there the moment they came out. I think it was one of the very first applications that was non-industrial, and that I was able to track down. Before that, we found some DC motors that were traditional copper coil type. That's where the whole idea of them (Streetly) wanting to put DC motors in there came, out of my experience in messing around with little electronic gadgets and projects, pulling things apart, and messing with them in my dad's workshop. I was able to envisage what would resolve that AC motor problem was to have DC motors. There were very small ones in existence, but never really anything strong enough to run a machine like a Mellotron, nothing with that kind of torque at that time. That was the obvious move, the first move that I had to make in terms of stabilizing the Mellotron. The pre-amps were all valves (tubes) and really microphonic, so that you could just tap the top of the Mellotron cabinet close to where the pre-amp was located at the back of the center, and you would have it coming through your speakers. That's a major fault with that, so consequently you would get certain sounds that would be spoiled by it.

On the rigors of touring with a Mark II:

I think the units were pretty strong. I never actually ever had a tube go out, which is amazing. The problems we really had were more mechanical, and once the DC motors were in and solved that problem, then we started to look at the mechanics, how the machine held up and things like that, the spring version versus the Chamberlin rewind system. They both had merit, but unfortunately, Chamberlins mechanically were not well built at all. For every screw that was there, there were three or four other holes where they tried first. There was a lot of sticking, and things like that. I had a couple of Chamberlins and I tried improving them, and did some various experiments with them, and actually did end up designing and building a couple of my own machines, but never finished them. I got quite far along, even having a couple of my own keyboards made in England. Other things took over at that point, and I think it was right about the time that I decided to come and live in America. That would have been the end of '73, beginning of '74, which was right around the end of the Moodies' world tour. It was the summer before that where I'd spent a lot of time working on my own version of the machine, trying to make it small, portable, light, but as tough as nails.

I've seen Justin Mayer's J-Tron and tinkled it once when he first built it. With the electronic things, the electronic samplers versus the audio tape sound, which is what the Mellotron is when you think about it, the difference is that in the perfection of the digital versions and everything, it's very wonderful and it sounds exactly like an orchestra, but the Mellotron didn't sound like an orchestra. It sounded something like an orchestra, but it wasn't the familiar orchestral sound. It just had certain qualities that made it different, and I think it's great that complete orchestral amateurs, like myself, made things happen and did things that were probably not in the orchestrator's book. We would do unorthodox fingering and intervals and all those kind of things. One of the most useful things for me was being able to use the VFO to slow down and speed up the pitch. I really enjoyed that, and it was something that, for some reason, I feel came from something deep within myself. It's the kind of person I am, I suppose.

When I was a boy, the stars and the universe were all of great, great interest to me, and became very much a part of my life. I was also a reader of science fiction. When I was not bound at school, I was Mikey the Moonboy, because I was always talking about planets, outer space, space travel and space ships.

I must admit I cannot include the 400 in the family of Mellotrons, in terms of it sounding like a Mellotron and performing like a Mellotron. The 400 is somehow a black-and-white photograph of a colorful Mellotron; it just has no color. It appeared they had somebody re-EQ the recordings, made copies, and then used them, trying to make up a set that would work for the 400. They thought they were improving it, when in fact they were actually ruining the overall sound and feel. There was something not right about it, but the Mark V was great. I love the Mark V. The Mark V sounded just like a really good Mark II.

Onstage, I exclusively used a Mark II. In the studio, I used a combination of Mark II, 300, and Chamberlin on occasion. The others never made it into the big time; they were always experimental. They just didn't seem to contain the basics of what the Mark II had, but that Mark V really did it. And of course, by then they (Streetly) cottoned onto the transistor amplifier cards and NAB equalization cards that I'd procured. They were new at that time. These cards were only 2" by 1", and 19-volt DC power supply, very clean, and were really good transistors. The EQ card followed the NAB curve very, very well. They sound just as good as the tubes do, without the microphonic effect. That's what the Mark V really ended up as being. It was a Mellotron with the DC motors, the transistor cards and NAB equalization card. That was directly out of my improvements to my machine, and then sending my machine to the factory to be mechanically checked, things like that. They would just pull off the ideas from what I've done that would appear in the next version, so I felt really nice about that. Well, they should have given me one at some point, don't you think?

On mechanical failures during concerts:

It's been played up much more than it actually happened. Really, about a handful to two handfuls of incidents occurred in the whole time, at the very most. A majority of them were completely fixable and were repaired by Mike Keys, the road manager, and me. Between the two of us, we would get it up and running pretty soon. There were two or three times that were pretty bad. I honestly don't remember us not being able to go on because of the Mellotron, in terms of canceling a show. I don't think we ever did that; we always got it going. One incident I distinctly remember happened at the Fillmore East. We got there, and it turned out there had been a bomb scare, and so they'd done a big sweep of the building. Anyway, they said it was OK, and lo and behold, we start up and I think we were into the 3rd or 4th number and something happened. Either a Coca-Cola spilled into the top of the machine, or something like that happened. I quickly got the back open, and I was down on my back and checking the tapes, and whatever. There was a light show going on at the same time, too, so what they ended up doing was they started showing cartoons while I was on my back fixing it.

On recording the Mellotron:

The tracks were overdubbed usually twice, once left and right, for the most part. Occasionally we'd do a little bit more if I wanted something special, or had something special in mind. I had completely different recordings made for the Mark II, other than the stock Streetly sounds at one time, but they never worked out well. As a matter of fact, I threw the 1" master tape away several years ago. It had already melted and was of no use anyway. It was not salvageable, and there wasn't anything brilliant there. I should have gone and done it again. Once again, it was still the magic of those original sessions. It's just the way they were recorded, the amount of zip that was there, and all of the little things, all of the nuances that collectively produced that particular set of tapes.

I only really used half-speed brass on "Question," in terms of it being set down at a pitch and then playing it, you know. The brass was used in "I'm Just a Singer in a Rock and Roll Band," but it was not slowed down. It was only "Question" where it was really predominantly used. I remember doing the end of Timothy Leary ("Legend of a Mind"). That very last note is one of those brass notes, and I tuned it down right at the end. That's another thing, and the reason that this is not really documented, is when you're doing things like that, you don't think for a minute that anyone's going to care, especially 30 years in the future. It's strange, some people actually do get it together and document everything they do. That's wonderful foresight, but I'm afraid my mind was more on what was actually happening, as opposed to trying to make capsules for the future. I think that when you're on a roll like that, and all of a sudden you've got a musical career that's taking off big time, those are the last things that you're thinking of. That would be the thing that really good management would take care of, and that's one thing we never had. And hence, that's why there's so little TV or film offered to us—performances and live shows and all of that is absolutely minimal compared with other bands of our reconciling ability and stature. It's just amazing. It was just one of those things that we made it in spite of our managers.

The only stuff I know that is not being seen, not even by me, is all the stuff that Peter Jackson shot on 8 mm. He's got a whole bunch of stuff, but I don't know what he has in mind to do with it. Actually, there's that stuff on the "Hullabaloo" video, where we were doing "Go Now." And there's also some great stuff on "Ready Steady Go," live stuff. One day we did "What'd I Say" with the Supremes standing on top of my piano and Smokey Robinson and the Miracles in a half circle behind us. Where's that footage? Come on, Dave Clark, where's that footage? There's just so much stuff out there that has been passed over. We never did American TV. That's because we lost our visas because of internal business problems with certain business people in New York, who have their finger in the customs and immigration pocket, if you know what I mean. It was in retaliation to some of Brian Epstein's dealings, because there were certain groups of people in America who wanted the concessions to the Beatles, and Brian Epstein wouldn't let it go. Consequently, they were penalized by this organization. We were, unfortunately, pawns in it, because when we arrived for our first American tour with H1 visas, they were taken away and made into H2 visas and we had to pay money to come in the country. We couldn't do TV, so all we could do are gigs and little radio interviews.

***On the minimal use of the Mellotron on his first solo album,* The Promise:**

It actually was wanting to distance myself from the Mellotron more than the Moodies' sound, because how could I distance myself from the sound that I really produced, you know? The Moodies' sound is very much Justin's songs and my arrangements, and you know that's the meat and potatoes of it, and the rest is peas and gravy, and dipping bread or whatever, when it really comes down to that. I wouldn't really want to get away from what I've done there. It was really more of giving myself a break from it, just so I would have a chance to see what else I could do. It was like wanting to stretch a little bit, as opposed to if I did everything with the 'Tron again, then I keep falling into the old habits. I was trying to break some of that, trying to break some new ground for myself. That was the motivation there. But of course, I came back around to it because I could fall back in love with it so easily. I think by being away also I realized that there were other musical things that I really wanted to get into that were not possible with the Moodies. There was a brand of music that we all brought something to that made it what it was, and there were certain things I just couldn't seem to get to happen. That would be evidenced by something like "Lost in a Lost World," for instance. The basic rhythm of that, for me, was to be even funkier than we were able to get it. I really wanted to get it looser, funkier, more rhythmic, more percussion, those kind of things. I wanted to experiment more in that area.

On the disposition of his various Mellotrons:

One of my Mark V's was lost in the Indigo Ranch fire. I sold some of the Mark II's and gave some away. By the time I got the Mark V's, it was like, this is it, this is mine, this is my Mark II. That's what it was, it was just that they finally got around to making my machine, which you know, I made the Mark II into. Finally they actually produced one as opposed to it being a machine that got a lot of fixes in it. I felt it was time to let them (the Mark II's) be moved on and let other people have the enjoyment of them as opposed to letting them rot in a storage shed. I was not about to get those out again, once I got a couple of the Mark V's. On those Mark II's, there would be distinguishing marks in exactly what kind of line amps and motors and things were in there, and whether the selector buttons were standard or multi-colored. I think I had black and white ones. I switched them around so that I had a more easily recognizable pattern of buttons to switch instead of four buttons all being the same color. It was like I need to do something that simplified this. If you hit the wrong button with the Mark II, you're waiting, what, 35, 50 seconds or something for the cycling to stop before you can start again and get someplace where you need to go. Once you started cycling, you had to wait until the end, so if you made a mistake halfway through a number, and I would, believe me, I was flying by the seat of my pants. I would cycle one side while I was playing the other during a song. That was pretty dangerous. The cycling motors were the biggest purveyors of major disasters, because if the cycling motor decided to stick at the wrong place, or at some times actually in between two sounds, you had it, you were basically out of business. And that was like, "Stop the show. Everybody go to the kiosk and get yourself a coffee and an ice cream and we'll try and fix it." Take the chain off, pull them back around by hand, put the chain back on, something like that. That was pretty bad. That, and liquid in the top, those were the two biggest problems after the AC motor problems. It's funny when I think about it. It's amazing that we actually did what we did, and with so few breakdowns. Like I said, there really was not more than perhaps a dozen times and of most of those, only two or three serious ones out of that. The others were fixable in anywhere between three and, say, fifteen minutes.

On his Mark II sounds:

The bread and butter sounds were the strings, the flute and the brass sounds. Those three we used so much. They were the ones that represented the three sections, strings, brass and flutes, woodwind and anything else that I could find. I would throw an organ in on the left hand side a lot too. I would do a lot of swooping with the pipe organ sound. A lot of the slide effects were with the pipe organ. Do one, and then double-track it, or something, or have someone else hold the chord on the right and then I'd hold the left and then do it. Do that kind of thing to make things happen. That was one way around it. When the band did "Peak Hour," it was definitely the pipe organ and Italian Accordion. I know I would switch from one track to the other. It was the track switch that I did that with and I probably went from track 3 to 2. On "Tuesday Afternoon," the intro sounds were strings and tenor sax. "Never Comes the Day" was a Mark 300. I remember that it was perfect for that. I also used it on "Watching and Waiting." "New Horizons" was Chamberlin, Chamberlin cello anyway. And, yeah, it could be 300 strings there too. And then "For My Lady," three violins...yeah, that's a 'Tron accordion in there. There were actually not many occasions where real instruments were used rather than the 'Tron—some, but not enough to confuse. "Just A Singer," we did that with half-speed brass. On *Seventh Sojourn*, "Lost In A Lost World" is definitely Chamberlin oboe. There would have been Chamberlin and Mark II on there. On *To Our Children's Children's Children*, "Floating" has pitch-bended vibes. That album was good. I liked the energy of *On the Threshold of a Dream*, too. It just had great energy. It was a great album. I played the upright bass on "Dear Diary."

Billboard just published a book that I was a part of, *Echoes of the Sixties*. I've got a 12-page chapter in there. The book showed up in all the Borders' bookstores, Barnes & Noble, and everywhere. I believe it's doing fairly well. I've just been so, so busy with so many different things that are happening right now. I'm still very much a family man, you know. I've got two of the boys at home.

Ian McDonald (King Crimson, McDonald & Giles, Foreigner, solo artist)

Ian McDonald

Hearing the Moody Blues was probably the first time I heard a Mellotron. They kind of beat us (King Crimson) to it. Although we didn't want to emulate the Moodies' sound, I recognized that this was something that I wanted to use because I had a certain amount of orchestral background. I was interested in classical music, and various other forms of music, had quite a wide range of experience, and I saw this as a way of incorporating different, and more sounds than the standard guitar/bass/drums, etc., into the band. Basically, that was pretty much the only thing around where you could do that. I mean it was the only way we could do it, so it was a natural thing, even though the instrument itself wasn't really designed to be used in that context, or on the road or on stage or anything. In fact, it was just sort of a thing to entertain your friends in the front parlor, which is really what it was designed for.

There are certain drawbacks with the instrument. They had their limitations, but you have to sort of learn to work with them. I did recognize that it was something that we could definitely use, and it sort of befell me to actually be the guy to try to figure out how to use it, how to get the best out of it. The Mark II's we used were totally factory, totally stock. I used to use some of the rhythm tracks in our improvisations because one of the things that Crimson was known for, and best at, was the sort of spontaneous group improvisations. I used to draw upon some of those pre-recorded rhythm tracks, etc. on the left hand side, and some of the block piano chords—it was a seventh or diminished chord, or something like that. I used to use the piano setting, the rumba end/finish, and various other things, and the Bungalow Bill beginning, that sort of thing just to add some humour and some variety to the improvisations. But the instrument was basically stark, and we kept the right hand as it was made. Of course, that in itself is a limitation, because as you probably know it has a fairly limited range. It's only got three octaves or something, and you know that limitation when you're doing an improvisation. I used to do it in this thing called "Mars," which was sort of a climax of our show, and this intense sort of piece, building to this incredible sort of climax. It was difficult because of the limited range of the keyboard to kind of keep this thing building and building, because it doesn't go that high, so that part of the way that I had to try and work within the limitations was to try and keep it exciting within a fairly limited range. I think a good example of that is the "Mars" from the "Epitaph" box set of Crimson from the Fillmore East. It was quite a good version. I start off very quiet, with string settings, just string pads, and then at some point I switch into the brass sound for the melody. It's the same brass setting that I used on the album *In the Court of the Crimson King* at the end of the song "Epitaph." The brass sound comes in there at the coda of the song. I think it's very effective. I think it's a great sound, one of the more effective sounds on the Mellotron, and you probably recognize it coming in at the end of "Epitaph." That's the same setting I used on "Mars" as well.

I recorded the Mark II through a Marshall or Hiwatt stack, whatever we were using at the time. A great big double stack of Marshalls or Hiwatts in a fairly large room, and miked at about 25 feet, so it definitely wasn't direct into the board. It gained a bit of ambient sound, and it had a closer similarity to our stage sound. As far as equalization, probably not a lot because I think the Marshall, or whatever it was, was probably adding some equalization. Other than that, we probably went straight into the board. We were only working on eight tracks, but I used to try and have at least two tracks of Mellotron, and sort of undulate the faders when we were mixing to give some kind of warmth and motion to the Mellotron, as opposed to just having a static, flat Mellotron sustaining in the background. So even though it's really not that audible, you get that sense of movement to the Mellotron you certainly wouldn't normally get if you were just plugging it straight in.

On purchasing the original KC Mark II #113 with his uncle's loan:

We had a meeting and said we need to equip the band. He said, "All right, this is what I'll give you," and he didn't question it, he didn't get involved, he didn't know about anything, let alone Mellotrons. He was a step-uncle. Basically, he was good enough to invest or finance enough money for us to equip the band. It wasn't just the Mellotron. He put up enough money so that we could buy a good set of drums, double Ludwig drums, amplifiers, and a couple of Mellotrons, and also to rehearse for a couple of months without having day jobs. He put up enough money for us to get started. It didn't provide any kind of income. We were still struggling, but at least we had equipment and rehearsal space. And that's pretty much what that was for. It wasn't just the Mellotron, it was the band's equipment, so we're very thankful to him.

The Ian McDonald flute was a request from Martin Smith (of Streetly Electronics). I recorded it in my apartment here in New York. There's an entranceway, a little foyer, and I set up a Neumann U-67, with the assistance of a friend of mine who's also a flutist. You wouldn't think so, but it's actually very difficult to give fresh samples of an eight-second note, just one after the other. It actually required someone else to help me do it, because I needed him to conduct, and to cut me off after eight seconds. It's not something easy to do by yourself, but I wanted it to sound nice, at least to sound better then the original Mellotron flutes.

The last time I used a Mellotron was probably when I left Crimson. I don't think I've used one since then. With Foreigner, there was one version of "Cold as Ice" that had strings added, the single version, and then maybe there in the bridge section, but no, it definitely wasn't the Mellotron on that sound. It might have been something that Al (Greenwood) was using. It definitely wasn't a Mellotron, but I know Al had an Orchestron, which he may have put on there.

When I left Crimson, I left the Mellotrons behind, and also there would have been such an association with the group had I used a Mellotron. We (Ian and King Crimson drummer Michael Giles) wanted to sort of separate ourselves, and I had the opportunity to have real strings anyway. I probably wanted to distance myself from the Mellotron at that point. As you know, they can be a bit difficult to play. In those days I was sort of known as a Mellotronist. I used to see it in the papers, "Mellotronist Ian McDonald," but I wanted to show people that I wasn't just a Mellotronist, that I could actually play other instruments. That's probably the thinking behind there. I'm actually going to be playing on an album that Mike Giles has been recording now over the last few months.

In fact, I've got to go to London in July, in about three weeks' time, to play on some tracks, put some flute and sax on a couple of things. It's not a "McDonald & Giles" album, but I will be on his record, and of course, he played on my solo album. There are some things I'd like to do to the original *McDonald & Giles* album before we go ahead and do another one. I want to remaster it, and possibly remix it if I get the opportunity, because there are some things that bother me about it. In fact, I have a computer here, and put "Birdman" into the computer, and I did some editing on it. It's a vast improvement, basically taking out a lot of the silences and tightening it up. I took about 11 or so seconds out of it, and overlapped the drum break that comes after the beginning of the building section, overlapping the last chord of the previous section. I did that on the computer, and it makes so much difference to keep the thing moving. I'm actually quite proud of "Birdman" as a piece of writing; I've just always wanted to tighten it up, just take some of the gaps out of it. I'd like to have an opportunity to do that, and re-release it, and then perhaps if I can do a few things like that, then we can go ahead and do another "McDonald & Giles." And I'll use a Mellotron. A Mark II.

On the November 1969 gig at Chicago's Kinetic Playground where a Mellotron Mark II was lost in a disastrous fire:

I know I remember we were trying to dry equipment out with hair dryers all night so we could play the next day, and all this sort of thing. Because the Fire Department had just strewn water all over our equipment, you know, it was just terrible, what a mess. Well, you know the trons were not built for the road. They would go wrong. That's why we had 2 or 3 with us all the time. It was guaranteed that you'd have to keep working on them, and in the early days, there were voltage problems. When the rest of the band was playing, the pitch would sort of go down, so I believe we had some kind of modifications done. We only had two roadies, and they're tough things to get around. I used to enjoy playing it onstage, actually, and there was this spring reverb unit on top of the Mellotron that I used to crash down on to create the explosions at the end of "Mars." It was fun. It was the sound of the times. Of course, it was before any kind of synthesizers, any kind of string ensemble, string sampler, or any other kind of string sound, so it was impressive at the time. People hadn't really heard anything like that.

A lot of groups used the 400 model, which I personally never thought sounded as good as the Mark II. I think they (Mellotronics) sort of made a cheap road version or something like that. Probably took out some of the mechanics to make it more reliable. But I just don't think they sounded the same. The transistorization thinned out the sound, and I just never cared for them particularly. I mean they're useful, but I really think you can't beat a Mark II.

Did I use Mellotron on "I Talk to the Wind"? Well, I can give it to you from the horse's mouth. There isn't one on there. I can tell you what there is. There are live clarinets, which is what I played, and real flutes, piano, bass, and that's about it. And some electric guitar from Robert (Fripp). No, definitely no Mellotron on "Talk to the Wind." There is, however, some Mellotron on "Moonchild." There's no string pad, there's a single string line back of the verses in "Moonchild." And also there's one line, or possibly two very short lines of Mellotron flute that I combine with a recorder that follows one of the vocals. That's what that is. I'm actually very fond of the Mellotron string line in "Moonchild." It's very subtle, but it's very effective. It's very operative. And I think it helps create an atmosphere of this sort of "willow pattern" atmosphere, as we used to call it.

Playing one note and having it sound fantastic—that's probably one of its best uses actually because of doing single line stuff. The other problem in playing chords is that the notes only last 7 or so seconds. That's another kind of nice use of the 'Tron, actually taking a lead, taking a solo, like the first solo of "In the Court," and that was very useful, and of course the electric harpsichord, which was not a Mellotron, but a Baldwin electric harpsichord that just happened to be at Wessex Studios just lying around. "In the Court" itself, there's just the string setting, except, of course, for the sort of cacophony/reprise thing at the end, which is all Mellotron of different settings. I think we have a couple of tracks of the Accordion setting on the left and right, giving it that sort of gritty sound, and other brass sounds. Basically, it's all Mellotron.

Some of the sounds within the 'Tron itself were out of tune with each other. That's synonymous with Mellotron. I mean the B note on the strings is always out, and various others, and I think that's part of the charm of the instrument. I think that's why it sounds like a Mellotron, because it is virtually out of tune with itself.

On the new sounds available from the Streetly library, such as bass clarinet, piccolo, recorder, French horn:
You know, I would enjoy using stuff like that, and they're probably better recorded, they're probably not as out of tune as the original ones. In fact, I offered to do a saxophone track, but I think he (Martin Smith) used Mel Collins. For some reason, saxophones tend to sound cheesy on this type of thing, I don't know why it is. Or every type of synthesizer that has a saxophone sample, something about it just doesn't transfer well, whereas bassoons and oboes and things like that sound fine. I don't know what it is. Even clarinets sound pretty good, but saxophone samples just sound really cheesy.

I spoke to Robert because I knew (King Crimson's Mark II) #113 was coming on the market. My studio and a friend really wanted it because of its historic value, he was very into vintage instruments, and especially vintage instruments that have some kind of history. You know, I basically relinquished the Mellotron when I left the group, even though it was sort of technically mine, and so I would have been buying my own Mellotron back, really. I'd love to have a Mark II again. It's not at the top of the list of things that I must have, but I would certainly at some point like to get one.

Rick Wakeman (Strawbs, Yes, solo artist, sessions)

I first became aware of the Mellotron when I did a session for a band called Junior's Eyes at Morgan Studios in North London. The studio had just opened (1968) and what became the bar was then the studio. Tony Visconti was producing and I was booked to play Hammond organ. In the corner of the studio was one of the original double manual Mellotrons that had just been delivered. Between takes, I played around with it and got to know its little quirks. What I really remember was being knocked out that here were sounds (albeit just the three) that had hitherto never been capable of reproduction with any keyboard.

It's true that Mellotrons were never really made for the road, and were a constant nightmare. Tuning, poor quality motors and tape racks, plus absolutely no back-up from the company, made it one difficult instrument to have on tour. . . and I used to take six; four for use on stage, and two for spares. If two on-stage instruments managed to finish the performance without spewing tapes out the back, then it was classed as a good night.

Jon Anderson hated their unreliability, and to that extent, so did I, which was probably where my initial love for the instrument back in the late sixties waned and turned into abject hatred!

I never exactly bolted together two M400's. They were totally dismantled and a new one-piece shell was made from the original woodwork, along with strengthened frames and new tapes, which we recorded ourselves. With nil back-up and support from the Mellotron company, there was very little other choice!

I used to have no special way of recording the Mellotron, although I did have a technique for playing the instrument, which to the best of my knowledge, nobody else used (and, as I'm unlikely to divulge what it was, nobody else in the future is likely to!). In the studio, it was always double-tracked, one track having board echo, and the other, a fairly fast repeat echo.

As mentioned before, the Mellotron was a night-mare to play: lousy touch, no control, always going out of tune, and badly built. It goes without saying that they were a nightmare on the road.

When I burnt the last Mellotron I had, to be fair, it was just a rotting wooden shell—a severely warped and battered frame, and knackered tapes. I did feel though, as the flames leapt skywards, that I had at last paid Mellotrons back in some small way for the years of hardship they had imposed on me! Having said that, "Space Oddity" and "Heart of the Sunrise" would just not have been the same pieces without the instrument, so let's call it a provisional cremation rather than a ceremonial burning.

The Birotron cost me over £50,000, and I don't even have one. It was the most obvious develop-ment to stem from the Mellotron, but as we reached fulfillment, some nasty professor invented/discovered the chip, and that was the end of that. *(Author's note: The Birotron, a joint venture by Rick and Dave Biro, was a compact tape replay instrument that ran on eight-track tape loops.)*

I honestly don't have any particular anecdotes about the instrument. It was lousy on every gig I ever did with it, but I wouldn't have swapped them on stage with anything else, funnily enough. Now even I can't answer that one for you!

As regards the Mark VI, I have to say I would undoubtedly use one on upcoming recordings, especially that of the new album that Keith Emerson and I are putting together, but that's up to them (Mellotron Archives) if they want to supply one or not.

Woolly Wolstenholme (Barclay James Harvest; contributor of "Deceivers All" to *The Rime of the Ancient Sampler—The Mellotron Album* CD; 400SM)

The band started in 1967, and we were playing around with conventional instrumentation of a rock band, but we also were mucking about with things like oboes and violas, and anything at all that would make a different sound. When it came to reproducing anything that sounded even remotely like an orchestra, the synthesizers of the time were not real, to us anyway, and the only thing that could do that was a Mellotron. We'd obviously heard it via the Beatles, Moody Blues, and Simon Dupree, so we knew about their existence. We found out about a man who was thumping to rent out a Mark II. I think we had it for a couple of days, but when it came to taking it back, he said, "I don't want it back," so we were sort of coerced into buying it. To buy it outright, allied with the fact that we'd rented it for a few days already, it wasn't that much more money just to have it completely; and that was really the start of the Mellotron thing. It was a kind of *fait accompli*. I think we paid twice as much as the rental and kept it, so it was a good deal in that respect. He found it to be an embarrassment, or he didn't want it. We used it on our early demos and our first single in '68.

We had that Mark II for about 1 1/2 years and thought that we couldn't gig with these machines because they're too heavy. No one wanted to buy it, and they were a little bit passé by that time; they were sitting in people's studios or lounges, but no one wanted anything to do with them. We said, "Let's throw it down the stairs," and we did just that a couple of times, plugged it in to make sure it didn't work, then claimed it on the insurance. Out of the money, we bought a 300 because it was easier to carry. The machine we tried to destroy went back to the factory, was repaired, and I think it's still out there somewhere, doing very well, thank you. With the 300, I had the same trouble with the fact it used to cycle when you didn't want it to, as it was a multiple station machine (like the Mark II). It would be plugged in before the sound check, and would go into a free-fall spin. Eventually, I had the plugs taken out, and ended up using the one set of sounds that I now have in the 400, which is strings and viola. What I have now are the 300A tapes [note: 2 violins, not solo notes as in the B tapes] and the Mark II sounds. Martin [Smith of Streetly Electronics] still has my 300's in the garage that still have the original tapes. The man they were supposedly sold to at one time sort of goosed them, and the restoration money would not be warranted—evidence of sacrificial Mellotrons, they've been cannibalized. I did have another Mark II, which also disappeared to the annals of history. I don't know where that one is either.

In the studio, other sounds I used were the flutes and the clarinet quite a lot, with other sounds coming in, like the brass, including some of the things I did in my solo work.

Fundamentally, I used 300A strings, occasionally supplemented by the Mark II, especially if it was a heavy song. For instance, on the song "After the Day," it has both models of Mellotron on it—a big, heavy King Crimson sort of sound. My trick for recording has always been the same—it's usually Mellotron and an organ, or some fusion like that. I used to do three tracks of Mellotron—one slightly sharp, one as concert as a Mellotron ever gets, and one slightly flat—thereby effectively making the sound bigger than it would have been with a single recording. The reason why an orchestra sounds big is because there are more people playing out of tune. If they were all completely in unison, it would sound like one person. It's the dissonance, the clangorous sound of someone not quite being on pitch, which makes things sound big, so that's why I apply it to the Mellotron. It's already in the Mellotron itself. As Bob Fripp says, tuning a Mellotron doesn't. They're already out of tune, and I compound the problem by making them more slightly out of tune. Tuning a Mellotron is an oxymoronic statement, like a diesel Ferrari.

I did use the Hammond spring reverb that was built into the 300. Occasionally, you went to whatever device was in the studio at the time. If you know the philosophy behind the 300, if you take the volume pedal down, the reverb stays—it leaps into a misty, ethereal sound, because the reverb return is still there even though you've reduced the signal. I'm not a great single line player. The chordal side of it is more the way I work. My playing technique is about complete, absolute suspension all the time. You start with E and then you play F# and put a D in there, then you might put a C in there, then you might put a G on top. Because of the limited eight-second play of the Mellotron, you have to have more notes down, then you have to refresh them by either putting them down again or putting another note in, so the whole thing fans out. As notes drop out, you replace it with another one somewhere. I believe in suspension, that is, anticipating the chord or being late behind it so you pretty much get all the notes going at once. In polytonality, the one you hear is the one that's appropriate for the part. If it were an E minor song, I would make sure that an F# was in there, perhaps a C somewhere, just to make sure it was always reaching or moving to the next chord before it actually happened. I used to call it "crabbing."

At one point, I was so fed up with the tapes either sticking or cycling that I used to start the show with a small fan heater blowing to warm the machine up. Another time, I was onstage and in the downtime between bands, someone smashed a glass on the Mellotron. I did the set, came off, and I was bleeding—the keyboard was covered in blood—a real rock and roll story. I was actually bleeding, and because it was dark, I didn't see or feel the blood because I was playing. I didn't feel the pain, my fingers were shredded, and the Mellotron was covered with blood. That would have been a great photograph.

The Rime of the Ancient Sampler was supposed to be tribute to the Mellotron, but on some tracks it wasn't the case. The problems were based on the idea that you can't take the sound then sample it and put it through processes until you don't recognize the instrument. It's a bit like saying you could record a violin and then modify it through devices so it didn't sound like a violin anymore. At the end of it, you're asking yourself, "Why do it?" I think that on some of the samples (tracks) on *Rime of the Ancient Sampler*—which was essentially not supposed to be about sampling at all—you couldn't hear the Mellotron even though they'd say "Oh, it's a Mellotron, but we've processed it so much it doesn't sound like one." I've never been inclined to take it out of its non-universe and move it to another place where it would not sound like a Mellotron. And I'm loathe not to take one up on stage—I've got a couple of gigs in Greece coming up in March and, because of technical reasons, I can't take a Mellotron out there. I'm going to have to sample it and put it into a keyboard, but it will still be exactly the same sound as the Mellotron—it will still last eight seconds—I won't loop it or anything like that. In effect, I will be still playing a Mellotron, or a Mellotronoid object. Its only redeeming feature is that it sounds like it does. If it were about technicality, reliability, or portability, you'd say, "Forget about it. It's really an anachronism. It should be in museums like a Ford Model-T." For me, the only great thing about it is its difficulty from the fact that it's a mechanical, very down-home engineered machine, technically very good, and has charm about it and the way it sounds. Therefore, I never get tempted to want to make it any different—a bit of reverb, a spit of echo, but not to change it fundamentally.

"Deceivers All" was a Mellotron track recorded before the *Rime* idea was mooted—it wasn't specially done to fit in with it. It was an unreleased track with plenty of Mellotron on it, and was typical of my output at that time. It wasn't out in any other form. Subsequent to that, it was put out again on *Songs from the Black Box*, which is a collection of my original solo album plus an extra track. I was pleased to give the track to Martin (Smith) for the CD because I didn't have the inclination or the mood to go back into the studio and do something else. It was a preexisting track. It did have lyrics, where most of the songs were instrumental or songs that weren't quite complete. In that case, mine was a genuine song as opposed to just a piece for demonstration. If you're going to have something that's ostensibly a Mellotron album, you can't have them playing second fiddle—bad pun there—it has to really be up front, and you say, "This is a Mellotron album therefore it's for the Mellotron." You can't say that, because I have this Mellotron, I can play the electric guitar or the mandolin, banjo, or saxophone, and say that's good enough—you still have to have a piece of music that is written at its own value besides that fact that there's a Mellotron on it. The problem with the original *Rime* was that they were not songs—it was a gesture If I do something (for the new CD), it would have to be a piece that exists in its own form, first of all, and then, of course, I'll use a Mellotron because it's a Mellotron song. That's my view of it anyway.

I agree that you can expose the Mellotron to the world through CD-ROMs, but I still believe that the Mellotron itself—a difficult thing to deal with, problematic, and needing regular maintenance—is like a real Ford Model-T. If someone made a new one that was faultless, I'm not sure it would sell or appeal the same way as the genuine article would. Or like a new Volkswagen Beetle—it's not built like the old one, it's been streamlined to death and probably works perfectly, but it will never occupy the same place in people's hearts as the original. And that is true of Mellotrons as well.

David Kean (Owner, Mellotron Archives, Mark II #123, M400 #245, Clear Mellotron #1, Oak Mellotron, T550, Mark VI #001, Chamberlin M1 plus M1 remote, Chamberlin Riviera, Birotron #007)

For me, initial exposure to the Mellotron came through Yes, King Crimson and Strawbs (*Hero and Heroine*) concerts I attended around 1972. That's what set the hook in me. And I bought a copy of King Crimson's *Lark's Tongues in Aspic*. My original Mellotron M400, purchased from a shop in 1973, had once belonged to the group Starcastle.

It was in 1989 when I tried to get a different Mellotron, M400 #245, repaired, and it was hard to find anyone who knew anything about Mellotrons at that time. I called Mellotron Digital and the phone was disconnected. I called *Keyboard* magazine, and they thought Mellotron Digital had just filed for bankruptcy. I called the bankruptcy courts. One thing led to another, and working through attorney Nathan Hightower, who I believe was a bankruptcy trustee for the state of Florida, he put me in contact with a guy named Bud Carr (in Florida). He was the owner of the building and was holding the entire inventory of parts, etc. for the rent money. When he found out I was interested in it, he said there was another guy interested in this stuff and that was Chuck Fedonczak. We kind of got into a little bidding war. When I found out that this stuff was for sale, the first thing that came to my mind was the Mellotron master tapes. To make a long story short, I lost the bid to Chuck. I had offered $7000 to Bud for the inventory. All Chuck wanted was all the modern R&D stuff. Jim Blair, myself, and others began a campaign and contacted Chuck on multiple occasions trying to obtain the tapes. After about two months, Chuck called me up and said, "Look, I am not interested in dealing with these people, I don't want to sell tapes, I don't want to try to make these tape machines work again, so why don't you buy this stuff for what you offered in the first place." I got that entire inventory that came from Mellotron Digital for $7000. That included about 20 tape frames, all the parts inventory, 1" masters, and some odds and ends.

I tracked down Leslie Bradley about two months later. His British master tapes were then being stored in an attic with a leaky roof, some of which were beyond saving. After some 30-odd hours of transatlantic conversations, I ended up purchasing from Les what he purported to be the entire collection of Streetly tapes, save for a few reels of Mark II masters. These included special tape sets done for the likes of Paul McCartney, Yes, Tangerine Dream, and Black Sabbath, among others. This is *the* Mellotron tape library. Subsequently, Markus Resch and I reworked the master tapes, using the best takes and saving them digitally and analog. We spent weeks on that project. To use a complete set from within one master tape was likely to yield several either extremely dull or extremely bright notes that stuck out like sore thumbs. My web site, **www.mellotron.com,** details this remastering process.

In 1991, when Markus Resch came on board, the first thing he did was take the SMS-3 (motor controller) and made it better, with the SMS-4. He then continued that with the SMS-5. The guy is just an absolute, dedicated maniac to the whole Mellotron world. Markus is also solely responsible for the development of the new tape frames. When it came to the Mark VI, it was a collaboration of ideas by Markus and myself, with Markus implementing them. He, Nicholas Berg (of the group Anekdoten), and his brother built those machines from scratch in Stockholm. Some of the further improvements on the Mark VI include more stable keys made by Klüger in Germany (who also make keys for Steinway). We also did another modification to the circuit that makes it even quieter than it was, having better RF rejection. Believe me, we've taken every Mellotron and Chamberlin out there on the planet and either bought one or borrowed one, and taken them down to their basic components. That's how the Mark VI came about. It's a labor of love. I still own the Mellotron business, but Markus is running it. I'm of the firm opinion that the Mellotron is a musical instrument/chaos generator that will never be duplicated because the mechanism is so responsible for such a wide range of multiplicities – of chaos, basically. There's no way of reproducing it, and that's one of the things that's so nice about it.

A few things warrant clarification. First, I do not have the original Motherton, as I have dubbed it. Leslie Bradley's original double-decker tape machine, an absolutely ingenious device he conceived in a dream, is in the Museum of Science in London. His original tape-making machine at the Streetly factory had custom-made heads with a narrower guard band between tracks, which allowed for better mixing of tracks. All current tapes suffer from inherently weak track mixes (i.e., placing the track selector switch between sounds A and B). Nothing can be done about it unless somebody wants to take the time to custom-build a head stack, and that ain't no small chore. Second, there were actually two clear Perspex Mellotrons made by Mellotronics in London for the same London Music Expo. Interestingly, unit #2 has a stress fracture on the case in exactly the same place as my unit #1. The walnut 400 that's in the museum was built by Bill Eberline, and was built as a test-bed cabinet for the 4-Track. I have the only oak 400 that I'm aware of. The rosewood 400 that I got from Chuck seems to be Mellotronics-built, although no one really seems to know. I have a picture of the brand-new clear cabinet sitting next to the same rosewood machine, so I'm pretty sure that Mellotronics built it. Third, let me try to put to rest any controversy over who owns the Mellotron name. As you may know, patents and trademarks have to be renewed, and the trademark Mellotron name was abandoned at the time I acquired the Mellotron Digital Inventory. After wrangling with the Patent & Trademark Office, who claimed that name had become generic, I was finally able to get, initially, the secondary registration of the name, then subsequently the primary registration of the Mellotron name. Fourth, with regard to the Mellotron name itself, in an interview with Harry's son Richard Chamberlin, I found out that Harry hadn't heard the name Mellotron until the Bradley brothers' product hit the market. Additionally, conversations I had with Les Bradley revealed that the Mellotron name was already 'affixed' to the instruments that Bill Fransen originally presented to the Bradleys. One can only surmise that the name Mellotron originated with Bill Fransen.

Pierre Veilleux (The Musical Box (Genesis tribute band), studio musician; Owner of Mark II #258, M300 #046, M400's #709 & 745, Mark V #128)

Pierre Veilleux

I played in the Musical Box, which was a Genesis tribute band, for seven years. I was also doing my real work as a lepidopterist, and it came to a point where we were very successful, but it came to making a choice, so I decided to quit the band and go back to my butterflies. Since that time it has been quiet musically, but I'm beginning to rework, and just ordered new tapes for my Mark II, new banks of sounds.

I got my first Mellotron in 1980, when I was 18 years old. My older brother was listening to all those Genesis and King Crimson records, and I remembered that introduction to "Watcher of the Skies." I liked the ambience so much, and the whole scary, horror movie sound I was asking the question, "What is the instrument for that?" and people said it was a Mellotron, but no one knew what it looked like or how it worked. I began my search and found my first machine, which was a Mellotron 400 (#709) that belonged to Morse code, a group here in Quebec. It was not working well, and at that time I didn't know how to fix the machines. I contacted Mellotron USA in New York and bought tapes from them. I bought another machine, which I found in Windsor, in a place where you raise chickens. It was a wreck with fly excrement on it, a real mess, and paid about $75.00 for it. I brought it to my place, and with two machines, I was able to make one good Mellotron 400.

I really believed in the sound even at that time. In the store, the DX7 was very successful, and all my friends were asking me why I was buying all those old keyboards. It's because the sound was so rich. On the Mellotron, the recording on each key is so different from one to another–every key has its own personality. Some are good recordings, some are not good recordings, but all those mistakes make the personality of the machine. That's why I like to play that instrument, and like what I feel under my hands. I began to collect Mellotrons, and in 1995, I had up to 18 machines. In my apartment, I had about seven machines, and the rest were in a warehouse in LaValle, that my wife didn't know about. I bought and restored a lot of 400's, selling or trading about 20 of them. I needed parts, so I called David Kean (of Mellotron Archives), and he helped me to restore the machines.

I came to a point where I wanted to have the other models, which were more rare. Here, in Quebec, there were not a lot of Mellotrons that came here, so I began my search for other Mellotrons and was able to find a Mark II in Toronto. We came back with it, and I remember that I was not able to sleep all during the week because the machine was in the place–it smelled so good, it was in mahogany. So I began to play with the Mark II, and realized that the sound was a lot different from the 400's. I realized it was the Cadillac of Mellotrons. The smaller capstan of the 400 pulls a lot more funky than the big Mellotrons, because the Mark V, the Mark II, and even the 300 have big capstans, and are more quiet, more stable because the bigger capstan is able to take more load. My two favorite Mellotrons are the Mark II and the Mark

V. I call the Mark V Darth Vader because it's all black with all those white keys—it looks very impressive. Mine is the one used by Neil Diamond's band on the *Love at the Greek* album, and also the same one that was at Bill Eberline's house. I like the Mark V (acquired in 1996) because you can change the tape rack in it like the 400, and I have my left hand, which is my accompaniment section. I have some acoustic guitar, some vibraphone, and so if I sit alone with that machine, I can make complete melodies that you cannot do on the 400.

It's a love-hate relationship; sometimes you love them, sometimes you hate them. With the Musical Box, I carried three 400's, because we were afraid to have problems with one machine, so we had one as a backup. I had a Hammond organ, an ARP Pro Soloist, and an RMI electric piano, and never had problems with the 'Trons, but we had problems with the ARP, the organ, and even with the RMI. If you maintain them well, there's no problem. I was proud of them, and the people who used to interview us always asked to come up on stage and see the Mellotrons. We had notoriety as a band that reproduced the exact Genesis sound with the exact instrument of the time, including the Mellotron. I had a special mix to be able to play "Watcher of the Skies," and other things from the *Trespass*, *Nursery Crime*, *Fox Trot*, and *Selling England by the Pound* albums.

I also did some research to make some modification on the keyboard itself. The original adjustment on the keys is about 2 turns on the pinch roller and 1 turn on the pressure pad. The first thing I thought when I touched a 400 was that it was like playing a marshmallow. You're playing in the rubber (of the pinch roller), so you have the limitation of not being able to play fast. And when you press a key, especially on something like the flute sound, sometimes you're going to hear a 'click' sound at the beginning. I was a little tired of that, so I began to try to find a way to make the keys play a lot faster. I began to move the position of the pads and cam, as well as changing the tape rack a little, and was able to reduce a lot of the friction in the machine and remove the key 'click.' Instead of 2 turns on the pinch roller, you now need only a half-turn, and the action becomes so light. I came away with a keyboard that you can play faster than a Hammond organ. I called John Bradley (at Streetly Electronics), who tried it on the Skellotron. John and his dad, Les, thought it was amazing, so for me it was like an endorsement of my modifications. After that, John began to incorporate it in his Mellotron restoration work. Jean Michel Jarre had it done to his Mark II and is very pleased with it. I think Dave Kean uses it in the new Mark VI, but I have never seen one, and haven't talked to Dave in a while.

I'm really attached to the machine and to the sound. I have memorabilia—all the brochures, the promotional sheets, advertisements in different music magazines—all the things that were around the Mellotron at that time. I once went to a place where there were farmers playing country music with a Mellotron on stage that they were not using, so I bought it. I found a mint 300, still in its muff cover, just a half an hour from here, that had been sitting unused for about 25 years, so I grabbed it up. Now I have a collection that is very representative of all the models. John (Bradley) came here and was very impressed with my collection. I tried to buy a Mellotron 4-Track, and know where one is, but the guy doesn't want to sell it. There were only four made. I think it's an important machine because there's lot of innovation in it. There were only two or three known T-550's made. I also had an SFX machine (#00015), the big gray machine with all the sound effects, which I recently sold back to John and Martin (at Streetly).

Gordon Reid (musician, composer, contributor of "Julia" to *The Rime of the Ancient Sampler—The Mellotron Album* CD)

When I was in 3rd grade (or thereabouts) in the late '60s, I occasionally heard records by bands that my parents didn't want me to hear, and some of these had a wonderful, evocative sound on them. I didn't know what the tracks were, or who the artists were, but quite a few had this amazing sound, and I fell in love with it. (The two I now remember best are Traffic's "Hole in My Shoe" and "Blackberry Way" by the Move.)

It wasn't until years later that I discovered that what linked these records was the instrument making the sound. I'd never heard the name "Mellotron" but a few years later, and like everybody else of my age group, I started listening to Pink Floyd, ELP, Yes, and Genesis. Again, there were these very distinctive sounds that Yes and Genesis made, and Floyd and ELP didn't. By a process of elimination (reading the record sleeves) it became apparent that the sound I loved was the Mellotron. Nothing else that could produce those string and the choral sounds and—apart from sampling a Mellotron—nothing since has come close to producing the same depth and emotion that the Mellotron creates.

A year or two later, in 1974, I bought my first synthesizer. This was a Korg 700, and I had this childish view that—because I now owned a synthesizer with loads of switches and sliders—I should be able to produce any sound with it. Of course, the Korg was monophonic and couldn't come within a million miles of producing ensemble-type sounds. This was when I realized that, like my heroes at the time (Keith Emerson and Tony Banks), I needed a range of keyboard instruments. And, of course, the one I wanted most was a Mellotron. Unfortunately, these were far too expensive for a boy still in school, so I didn't own one until 1981.

I answered an advertisement in one of the music magazines, drove halfway across the country, expecting to buy what I now know is a Mellotron 400, a nice, neat, manageable white Mellotron. Instead, the guy had a big, brown thing with two keyboards in his garage. I asked him, "Is that really a Mellotron?" And he said, "Oh, yeah. It's just a different type of Mellotron." Of course, it sounded just like a Mellotron so I bought it, having no idea that I'd purchased one of the three remaining Mark I's (#124). I took it home, and then found that it had all the stepper motors taken out and the tapes cut, so it was in effect converted into two 400's in a single case. Fortunately, the seller had given me all the stepper motors and the percussion bits and pieces (rhythm/fill tapes) in a cardboard box, but I never found the time to start restoring it.

I used #124 on a number of recordings, but I never gigged with it because it was far too heavy. I had just one guy who roadied and engineered for me, but we couldn't easily move it, and the rest of the band wasn't interested in helping.

I spoke to Les Bradley in 1982, and he told me that all the early Mellotrons went to famous homes. One ended up with the boyfriend of the Queen's sister, Princess Alexandra, and I think that Peter Sellers owned the same instrument at some point. All the others were sold to famous bands and well-known artists. Les was convinced that mine had been played on some famous recordings, but the early sales records had been destroyed, so he couldn't tell by whom or on what. Certainly, #124 showed signs of serious gigging, but it was by no means in a battered condition. In fact, I now know that it was in a lot better condition than most.

In about 1986 or '87, Nick Magnus and I sampled #124. If I remember correctly, the six sounds in it were the brass sound from Genesis' "Watcher of the Skies," a 15-voice choir, the 8-voice choir, a Hammond organ, a church organ, and one of the string sounds. We sampled these, with (at the time) a state-of-the-art 12-bit sampler, and put together a library for just the two of us. Shortly afterwards, we were approached by a company called the Engine Factory, and they sold these samples for a few months. I then started hearing my Mellotron on other people's material. Probably my favorite example of this is Marillion's *Brave*.

When I moved home shortly afterwards, I discovered that I couldn't get #124 into my new house because the doors were a bit too narrow, so it ended up sitting in my garage. I didn't want it to deteriorate, and I ended up advertising it in '88 or '89—"free to a good home." Eventually a guy named Russ Fiton offered some digital gear in part exchange, and I jumped at the chance. In retrospect, this was a really daft thing to have done. If memory serves me correctly, I paid £425 for it, which is about $700, and gave it away for nothing. So I was both fortunate at the beginning and extremely stupid at the end.

Russ sold #124 to Dave Kean (of Mellotron Archives), and the next thing I knew it was over in the States, and Dave Kean was on the phone to me saying, "I understand that you've still got the stepper motors for this." I dug out the old cardboard box (which still had the bits in it), packed everything carefully, and sent it to him. He then sold #124 to somebody (but I have no idea who that was). Finally, this owner sold it to Jerry Korb, who got in touch with me through the Mellotron forum. In the end, I'm not too sad about having given it away, because Jerry has done a fantastic restoration job on it. It's gone to the best possible home. If I had kept it, it would never have been restored to its original condition.

Of course, after I had given #124 away, I quickly became desperate for another Mellotron. I was again very lucky because a friend told me, "I know somebody who has a mint 400 in its Protector Muff, and it's just gathering dust. I'm sure that he would sell it." So I jumped in the car, drove 50 miles, and there it was...exactly as promised. It was a beautiful instrument, with the classic string, flutes, and split choir tapes, still in its Protector Muff, and still with its delivery note from Streetly Electronics. Better still, the seller was happy for me to have it for £140, which was about $200. Sure, it's not the same as owning one of the three remaining Mark I's, but I will never let go of the Mellotron I now own.

On "Julia," Gordon's contribution to the* Rime *CD: Martin Smith (of Streetly Electronics) sent me a cassette of some doodling that he had done on his Mark II Mellotron. This included one melody which, to me, stood out from the others, so I contacted him and said, "Do you mind if I build a piece, starting with your melody, and then developing it into something of my own?" He said, "No, I don't mind," and the track was born. The first theme on "Julia" is the variation of Martin's doodle. People sometimes level one criticism at the track. They say that there's not enough Mellotron on it. But almost everything on "Julia" (apart from the drums and guitar) is Mellotron. All the brass sounds are Mellotron, the piano is Mellotron, the bass, I think, is Mellotron, even some backing guitar is Mellotron that we manipulated a little bit in a sampler. Unfortunately, too many people expect 8-voice choir, 3 violins, and very little else when you say "Mellotron," and they are often closed-minded to the other sounds that you can create with one.

I'm not sure whether I should admit it or not, but it's best to be honest: "Julia" was recorded using samples from my Mark I and from various 400s; it's not recorded 'live' from a single Mellotron. Nick worked incredibly hard to get to get those samples exactly right. He did this by taking the longest possible sample and using the Roland's "alternate" looping capabilities to move backwards and forwards within the file. He created a set of samples that had the characteristic spit at the beginning, and so much movement and change within the notes that they sounded remarkably authentic. We used these on "Julia" because Nick's studio is at the top of a narrow flight of stairs, and has quite a small control room. It wouldn't have been practical to get even a 400 (let alone a Mark I) up there. We agonized about this, but in the end we decided that, if we could fool Martin Smith or any of the other contributors who were playing Mellotrons, it was a legitimate use…and we did.

What I'm trying to say is this: the instrument is not the be-all and end-all. What's important is the music that you produce with it. If you can produce that music when playing the original instrument, that's great, and I love doing it…it's fantastic to stand with a Mellotron in front of an audience. But if you can produce the same, wonderful, emotional, evocative sound in a different way (in this case by creating a set of samples that are indistinguishable from the original) then it's equally valid.

I think that people lose sight that the important thing is the music. Like Hammond B3's and Minimoogs, Mellotrons are icons and rightly so. But they're icons that only a few people can own or have the opportunity to play. For everybody else, what's important is the sound and the music and how that music makes you feel, not the mechanism. If I can sample a Mellotron and use those samples in such a way that the music loses none of its soul or character, I think it's just as valid as playing the original instrument.

Along with many other Mellotron players, I discovered the spider-crawling-across-the-keyboard technique. I would listen to Rick Wakeman's playing on albums such as *Yessongs* and, although I didn't understand what was happening, I loved the sound as notes came and went within the mix. Later, when I bought my first Mellotron, I worked that out. With a little bit of reverb to smooth the transitions, I could release keys, let the tapes return, and cycle through the notes to create chords that lasted much longer than eight seconds. What's more, I could do this with just one hand, whilst playing other instruments with the other. I think that there's something incredibly organic, human, and musical about the technique. In contrast, it's too tempting when using string ensembles and early polysynths (I had a handful of these too) to find a chord, press the notes down and just let it sustain indefinitely. OK, the chorus units within these keyboards produce a certain degree of movement within the sound, but ultimately it becomes just an organesque sound that sustains for as long as you want. No orchestral player would play a sound like that, and no arranger would arrange a piece like that. So, because the Mellotron forces you to create movement within the sound, the 8-second limitation becomes a strength.

Eventually, I stopped playing the Mellotron for anything apart from my own pleasure, but I still find myself using the 'spider' technique on my polysynths, and I still think that it adds a lot to the music. So, in effect, I play my big modern, digital workstations like a Mellotron. That's quite a legacy.

John Hawken (Nashville Teens, Renaissance, Strawbs, Illusion)

I first became aware of Mellotrons around 1970 while I was with Renaissance. We were signed to Island Records and spent some time around the original studios in the converted church at Notting Hill Gate. Against the far wall of what I believe was Studio 1 was a huge old two-keyboard Mellotron. It looked most impressive and I very much wanted to hear what it could do. Unfortunately, it had suffered a severe attack of temperament (a condition I later became all too familiar with) and the inside of the machine resembled spaghetti junction!

It was not until three years later that I finally got to play one and it was something of a crash course. I had been invited to join the Strawbs and I duly turned up at a small studio near the Chalk Farm Roundhouse for my audition. After the usual pleasantries had been exchanged, Dave Cousins pointed me in the direction of a Mellotron and suggested that it might be a good idea if I became familiar with the instrument that had become very much an integral part of the Strawbs sound. After a couple of helpful hints from Dave, I sat down and attempted to "tickle the ivories." Disaster!

Nothing quite prepares you for the strange, disconnected feel to the keys accompanied by the hissing and fluttering of the tapes over the pick-up heads, followed shortly thereafter by a slight thud, then silence, as your eight seconds of sound are up. I felt distinctly uncomfortable (this was, after all, an audition) yet at the same time I was exhilarated by the huge and impressive sound pouring out of "the Beast." After a short period of familiarization I felt very much at ease with the instrument and appreciated the powerful effect it always had on an audience when properly amplified through the P.A. system. Unfortunately, at about the same time, I realized something else about Mellotrons. They do not like to travel. The slightest flexing of the cabinet and subsequent misalignment of tapes and heads would cause a Mellotron to produce sounds not unlike the squealing of small animals in extreme pain! Not conducive to a good performance!

We had the two Mellotrons strengthened with cross-bracing and corner brackets and this certainly improved matters. This treatment did not, however, address yet other foibles of this neurotic machine. It suffered a strong aversion to any change of temperature—and, oh yes, it required an absolutely stable power source (there were many jokes about the caretakers of the halls in question not pedaling fast enough).

One gig in particular stands out as being responsible for almost total meltdown of our two Mellotrons. It was an open-air concert in Phoenix, Arizona where the afternoon temperature rose to well over 100 degrees, and as luck would have it, that was the time we were due to go on. I had not hitherto realized how fragile recording tape is. Roll up and watch the tape racks shrivel before your very eyes!! On a good night, however, this seductive mistress would melt your heart and all would be forgiven. My favorite three-track tape consisted of Strings, Choir and Brass, and these sounds were a major part of the Strawbs sound as well as, later on, a major part of the Illusion sound (this latter band was a reincarnation of the original Renaissance). I personally owned a Mellotron up until I immigrated to the United States in late 1979. I stupidly sold it, dare I say, for a song.

Tony Visconti (producer—T-Rex, David Bowie, Moody Blues)

I first heard the Mellotron on "Strawberry Fields Forever." I immediately knew that the flutes weren't real, but no special effect, to my knowledge, could produce that fluttery sound, except maybe a wobbly tape. I wasn't far from right. I was a newcomer to London and working with my mentor, producer Denny Cordell, as his assistant. It wasn't long before we hired our own Mellotron and used it on some early Move recordings, but I can't remember which particular tracks. After the Beatles and Traffic used it first, everyone was using it. I laughed when I heard the tire screeches and flamenco guitar run used on "Back in the USSR" and "Bungalow Bill," respectively. Of course, the Moody Blues used it their way, too, with the *Days of Future Passed* album. By mid-1968 you could say that the Mellotron was overused.

I also used the Mellotron for T. Rex, which I played on a track called "Tenement Lady," the opener of *Tanx*. For the string sound the Mellotron would have to be tracked at least two or more times to smooth out the eight-second limitation. It was later confirmed that Mike Pinder also did this. The strings, on their own, were very thin and lo-fi. About three overdubs would start to approach "lush." The most characteristic sound was the click at the beginning of virtually any note, the point of contact with tape to playback head.

I would never try to replace real instruments with the Mellotron. I would make it obvious that it was one. I let it do its "thing." I had to EQ the harshness out, subtract around 2 kHz, about one or two decibels. This had a more pleasant effect rather than boosting high end, which would always boost more hiss. Sometimes you could get away with a little boost around 4 kHz. It depended on how worn out the tapes were. It was always frustrating to get that one dull note in the middle of some good bright ones. I always took a direct output from the instrument. I never miked the speaker. If possible, I would make use of the pitch bend facility and make the notes drop or rise in pitch whilst holding a chord, usually dropping it. Another good thing about the pitch knob was you could drop or raise the pitch of the instrument to play in a difficult key. For instance, if the key was F#, you could pitch it down a semitone and play in G.

Many times I have witnessed the mechanism go haywire and watch miles of tape being spewed out all over the studio wall. This always called for a celebration at the pub, whilst the roadies stayed behind and fixed it.

It (the Mellotron) was a big pain to record and maintain. Like all flavors, it eventually lost its charm and I was glad to see it go. Years later, I have sampled several different Mellotrons from the Moodies with a friend who works at Roland, Jan Paulshus. I selected the brightest notes and "stretched" them over a few keys rather than use every note, good or bad, for the sake of it. I've created "super" Mellotron patches that loop forever with no eight-second limitation. All the notes are in tune, too. I've recently acquired AutoTune for my ProTools rig and I was thinking of running my Mellotron samples through them once more to get them more in tune. The trouble with Mellotrons in the new millennium is that the tapes are getting old and wearing out. Sampling will at least preserve the sound before they all become unplayable. I have certain friends who would jump off the Brooklyn Bridge if that ever happened.

On the Moody Blues' Mellotrons:

I think they have two in storage, or maybe Mike (Pinder) took one and left them with one. I persuaded them to take one out for the *Keys of the Kingdom* CD. Instead of playing them, I sampled them and we played the sounds through an Akai S1000. The Mellotron strings you hear in their present concerts are from the samples that I made. Their chief road manager, Mike Keys, looked heavenward and sighed exasperatedly when I asked him to fire it up. He was amazed it worked. After I took my samples (by recording every note onto DAT tape, then loading the best notes in the Akai S1000), I told him he could put it away again. He replied something like, "Thank God for that!" Justin (Hayward) told me that they were unhappy with the original string sounds of the instrument, so they booked their own string sessions and made their own string patch. I don't know if they recorded anything else.

I have several friends who own them and they cherish their Mellotrons, belonging to the official club. As a producer, I have probably used more Mellotrons than my friends. I know the sound has lately come back and I'm so happy I made my samples because they are really hard to get a good sound out of. I must mention that I always felt the Chamberlin was a superior Mellotron and David Bowie still owns one. We used it extensively on several of his albums, including *Low*, *Heroes*, *The Lodger*, and *Scary Monsters*. I loved the saxophone sounds. We used that a lot.

John Wetton (King Crimson, Uriah Heep, Asia, Qango)

I first heard the Mellotron on Beatles records, but became more aware of the King Crimson/Moody Blues records in '68/'69, and thought it was just what rock needed to take it to a step closer to orchestra, i.e., to make "orchestral" noises that weren't—to give music size and melodic/harmonic pomp without the conventional sugary pop strings and woodwind of the day. In that respect, there was a huge "aha" (later to be "oh-oh").

Ian McDonald probably wrote the definitive Mellotron tune ("In the Court of the Crimson King"), and used the instrument in its best environment, i.e., unison with a third below (or above) to embellish. With King Crimson, we rehearsed for many weeks without the 400's, but when we did use them, they added another dimension to the music. By the time I joined King Crimson, Robert (Fripp) had a pretty good handle on the way to voice the instrument (an art in itself), and I learned a great deal from him. I still listen now to guys who play it like a synth, and it makes me chuckle—it is not a synth, it is not an orchestra, it's a fucking machine—of course, it's what's in your head that matters, but how you translate that to tape is a different story.

I totally agree with Mike Pinder in both aspects of his evaluation ("fell in love with the sound; as a machine, it was a pain in the rear"). We were held ransom by that instrument on so many occasions; it was hard in '72-'74 to imagine King Crimson without Mels, but we did on occasion perform even when the 400 did not. The 400 comes into its own in the voluminous hockey arenas of North America, where other instruments (bass and drums, usually) are swimming for their lives—the more tinny and cheesy the natural reverb the better for our mechanical friend. Each Mellotron comes with its own Gremlin, individual as a fingerprint, and just as difficult to detect, but also just as incriminating.

For me, voicing the Mellotron is crucial. It's ok to use straight triads on flutes ("Strawberry Fields") but disastrous on strings. Cellos are best only on single lines, and strings have to be placed very carefully, thirds and fifths well spread apart (e.g., I would play a "C" chord GEC, GCG, or CGC, but not CEG). You can jam the selector between two tapes for unusual combos. The eight-second transport is there merely to keep you on your toes, and remind the brain to keep those fingers changing position, rather like high-speed musical chess.

My only experience, and intimate relationship was with the Carpet 400 (#354). I shall give her a tender tweak next time I visit Robert. Maybe we could visit the soft furnishings department together and choose a new underlay for her, maybe even a shag-pile for the next millennium. *[Author's note: The Carpet 400 John refers to is the M400 covered in felt matted carpet that was used on King Crimson's* Islands *album, and Crimson's Fall 1971/Spring 1972 U.S. tours. It was sold to Uriah Heep, when John briefly joined the group in 1975, but eventually found its way back to Crimson ownership.]*

Nick Magnus (Steve Hackett band, solo artist, contributor of "Night of the Condor" to *The Rime of the Ancient Sampler–The Mellotron Album* CD)

Yes, it was an "aha" revelation! My first conscious recollection of the 'Tron sound was on the Rolling Stones' *Satanic Majesties* album, which my older brother used to play a lot. I was totally captivated by this weird sound; I didn't perceive it as being strings at all. It was unearthly and gothic, quite beautiful, and at the time rather at odds with my idea of what the Stones were about. I don't remember how I discovered it was a Mellotron. It was probably by deduction from the sleeve liner notes. Immediately after that revelation (the mid '60s) it seemed the Mellotron cropped up everywhere. The Small Faces used it on their *Ogden's Nut Gone Flake* album, the one with the Stanley Unwin narration, and I remember feeling very smug during the "Boy Blue freaked 'em all out on his Mellotrove" bit, knowing what he meant by "Mellotrove."

As with any instrument, your playing technique adapts to suit, or at least it should! Like everyone else, I adopted the "cyclic" approach to playing chords that lasted longer than eight seconds, i.e. cycling through the notes in the chord in such a way as to disguise any discontinuities of sound. In the studio I used reverb and delay to help with this, and on stage I used a Roland RE201 delay unit. One occasional studio "cheat" was to crossfade two overlapping tracks to produce a smooth transition for those extra-long notes. Using a swell pedal was also crucially important to give the performances some sort of dynamic realism. I never had any notable problems with reliability in the studio, but on stage it was a different matter, as explained later!

As mentioned above, reverb is a very important tool. I was thrilled the first time I played the 'Tron through a Lexicon 224; it seemed so smooth and lush compared to plate reverbs. One often used EQ treatment is to slightly back off the mids around 1KHz to get a silkier, more orchestral color. In those weirder moments, I've put the 'Tron through a vocoder, e.g. during "Tigermoth" on the *Spectral Mornings* album. There are also occasions when I mix the 'Tron strings with synth strings (in latter days, a Prophet 5 or MemoryMoog) for a really "Rachmaninov" texture. "Hammer in the Sand" from (Steve) Hackett's *Defector* album is a good example of this 'Tron-plus-Prophet sound.

I personally have never owned my own Mellotron, but all through the Hackett years I used Steve's Novatron 400. It was very much the center-piece of my keyboard setup, so I felt as if it was actually mine! It had a variety of tape frames which covered violins, 8-voice choir, male and female choir, 16-voice choir, string section, flute, cello, brass, and even Steve's voice going "Aaaah" (as taken from the NECAM voice loops featured on "Please Don't Touch"). I haven't yet seen a Mark VI, but its existence (and that of other machines like the J-Tron) show that the Mellotron concept is still alive and well, so I'm all for that!

Oh yes, I've had my fair share of on-stage Mellotron cataclysms. On two separate occasions I had the motor burn out in the middle of a show. Not a nice smell, that's for sure. At first I thought the smoke effect machines had gone wrong! There's not a lot you can do apart from switching the thing off and hoping the flames don't spread.

The other classic breakdown, which happened all too often, was the old 'sticky tape' problem. This would be caused by condensation on the tapes, generally from the poor 'Tron being subjected to alternating extremes of temperature—hot truck, cold venue, hot sound check, cold interval, hot gig. You'd be playing away, and notes would inevitably hit the eight-second limit. But when you released them to let them rewind, nothing would happen; the oxide had become a brown, sticky mush and the tape was stuck to the playback heads. I didn't have a specialist keyboard roadie, so whenever Steve's guitar roadie was free, he used to sit behind the 'Tron (with its back off) rewinding the tapes by hand, like some lunatic bell-ringer. It sometimes got so bad that I had to abandon the 'Tron and fill in on one of the other keyboards. Fortunately, we carried tape frame backups, so the next gig we could replace one if it was damaged beyond salvation.

On his contribution to the Rime CD, "Night of the Condor":

The answer to this may well cause cries of "Heresy!" For various practical reasons, I used samples—I've never had a problem with that, as the end result is the important thing. They are all samples that I've created and prepared myself very carefully from a variety of Mellotrons. Space was a prime consideration—my studio is fairly tight for space, so getting a real 'Tron in there would have been an insurmountable problem. Using samples also allowed a far greater degree of dynamic control, being able to draw detailed volume curves into the sequencer. It's analogous to using a swell pedal, but with far greater precision.

The *Rime* CD came under much criticism for its apparent "lack" of Mellotron. In fact, it's brimming with the stuff! One possible reason for this could be that a number of contributors opted for sounds not often associated with the 'Tron, and I too decided to include a few of those. To which end, "Condor" has Mark II and 400 Violins, String Section, 16-voice Choir, Female Choir and Flute from the standard repertoire, plus Piano, Nylon guitar, Vibes, and Boys Choir. The other sounds (not including drums) on the track were bass, electric guitar and a (Roland) D50. The 'Tron sounds were recorded in just the same way as I'd record the "real" thing: same EQ tricks, lots of volume changes, and, of course, a nice juicy reverb. In addition to my own "Night of the Condor" track, I also produced two of the other tracks, Martin Smith's "Engulfed" and Gordon Reid's "Julia."

Brian Kehew (Moog Cookbook; owner, Mark II # 125/M400 # 226)

I love the limitations of the keyboard itself, with short and heavy, tough-to-push-down keys. When I play on that keyboard, it's a really physical effort, as are playing the guitar and drums. Regular synth/organ keyboards are very nonphysical and no fun to play. Through the keys, I can feel the motor vibrations and the instrument seems more alive.

I long ago learned the "random one finger lift" during long held chords. This is the only way to stretch out the eight-second length. I think the unreliable stereotype of Mellotrons is not really necessary; in the '70's few people knew as much about their gear as we do now. We have better motor controls, maintenance, and information. I have had many Mellotron disasters, but mostly due to my own faults: Trying to move it downstairs by myself—leaving the rare UK power cord at home when recording...

Compression helps, but the critical aspect is a swell (volume) pedal. It really helps attacks and fades. EQ totally depends on the tapes and the desired tone. Personally, my best results come from running the Mellotron into an amp with a 12" speaker (which lops off some of the top treble end naturally) and some reverb. Spring reverb sounds "authentic" (12" speaker and spring is the essential Mark II sound), but I really can't say enough good things about the little Microverb (first model, not the 2 or 3) from Alesis. It's very natural and warm sounding. Beats out the Lexicon 224XL, plates, springs, anything! Also, my favorite sound is to play and record the part twice, then pan each one hard Left/Right. Each time you hit a chord, the notes stagger in slightly different ways and the textures that result are really nice, almost three-dimensional.

I have an M400S and a Mark II. I think the new Mark VI is great. I love the sound, and the pre-amp with balanced output is a great idea. I don't love the finish (the original 400's are beautifully unique) or the keyboard action, and I hate everyone devising ways to lighten/quicken the keyboard action. It feels "wrong" to me, like playing a guitar with tiny strings or a drum with rubber heads. The keyboard feel is one of the "rightest" parts of an old Mellotron. The Mark VI is probably the best tape instrument for a studio to own. It sounds very good, is reliable and likely to be useful.

Two stories—I live on the second floor (not numbered the same for Europeans, though). When I have to get my Mellotron 400 to a show or studio, sometimes I have to get it downstairs by myself. It's a heavy beast, so I came up with a trick. I get it to the concrete stairs, and then turn it upside-down onto a blanket. Then I can easily slide the blanket downstairs and the Mellotron rides with it. Only once, I was careless and the Mellotron skidded off the blanket and down the stairs! Ouch...

Second story—Once I auditioned for a band that wanted vintage and modern keyboards. I was using samples and analog synths and the Mellotron. For the complex song we were playing, I was given a tape and told to sample all the elements—guitar parts, drum fills, FX, voices, etc. The night before the audition, I was up late getting the "homework" done and the sampler ran out of memory! There was no way to load mid-song or expand the internal memory, so I was stuck. I took the tape, transferred it to 1/4" reel and then laced the tapes into unused notes on my Mellotron. It worked fine—and the singer was amazed to see and hear his voice come out of a Mellotron! I got the audition.

On acquisition of Mark II #125:

I was to meet Dave Kean (whom I first called when I got my M400) on his visit to L.A. We met when he went to Mitchell Froom's studio where Dave was to buy and trade some instruments. At one point, everyone was loading and unloading instruments, and there were about 3 Mark II's and two M400's on the sidewalk in Hollywood! We joked about putting up a "Yard Sale" sign and causing accidents all over.

As each person was organizing to take instruments for transport, they found out there wasn't room enough for one of the Mark II's—a newly refinished one in white. I offered to take it and hold it for a few days until the guy could come and pick it up in a larger vehicle. Dave Kean said he thought it would be OK with me to do so, and he believed it to be one of Genesis' Mellotrons. (They are one of my favorite groups, and one of the main reasons I've always wanted a Mellotron!) Eventually—the guy never picked it up, and I arranged to buy it "as is" from Dave. The trouble was, it had been taken apart for refurbishing and was in hundreds of pieces. Without a manual or visual model to work from, it was a slow task to redo it myself. I could only test-fit screws and cables to see where they "might have gone." Eventually, with Dave and Steve Frothingham's help, we restored almost all of it perfectly. I still haven't laced the tapes as I write this—it's a daunting task, and I don't want to approach it alone.

On the history of Mark II #125:

According to John Bradley (of Streetly Electronics), it was "born" a Mark I (the 25th) and typically converted to a Mark-II sometime later. After that initial birth, we lose track of it.

According to the person Dave bought it from, it came to America in early 1974. The American had wanted a Mellotron and somehow contacted the keyboard player of the band "Jonesy" about a trade. The Jonesy fellow wanted a Minimoog and could not find one easily in London, so they traded a Mellotron for the Minimoog (He thinks the initial contact was about late 1973, this is also one of the times when Minimoogs were really taking off). It seems this Mellotron had been "toured," as it had an original muff-cover, the speakers were removed (unnecessary weight, as the amps are too small for live use), and each side had only one bank of 3 sounds (no shuttling needed). These were the common modifications many bands—such as the Moodies- had done to their Mark II's for the road. The finish was white—likely the only one ever made so. It had been repainted by Mellotron Archives before I got it, but the original white paint is visible inside the cabinet and there was never any glossy veneer on the machine—just painted wood.

Genesis? Who knows? They seemed to be using M400s by 1973/74 and never used Mark II's again (that we know). Tony (Banks) evidently went through several Mark II machines. One in brown was bought from him in 1998. They owned one they bought from King Crimson (nicknamed "The Black Bitch") and there was one brown one (painted white) in 1973 on tour that had output jacks on the upper back panel. This machine is none of those, but there may be one more clue to its history: Terry Kelly had spoken to Les Bradley—at the time, the only surviving brother of the original family. Terry mentioned this white Mark II and Les said that only one white Mark II was made, and Tony Banks had it. If someone could only ask Tony about such things, but he hates Mellotrons even more than John Paul Jones!

Jerry Korb (owner, Mark I # 124, M300 # 037, JK-MK6 #001)

Unashamed to disclose my age, the Mellotron has been a part of my life since I first heard one in 1967, when I was 13 years old. That "aha" feeling was clearly felt, and STILL felt to this day. The local FM station in New York, WNEW-FM, featured famous DJ's like Scott Muni, Alison Steele (rest her soul) that featured lots of English prog-rock tunes of the era—the free-format radio station, a thing of the past I fear. Anyway, Scott once explained the workings of the Mellotron on the radio. I realize now that he attempted to describe the innards of a Mark II. Alison Steele called herself, "The Night Bird," and, after 11p.m., started-off her cosmic hour with King Crimson, early Genesis, Tangerine Dream, and of course the Moodies.

During the short time I joined a band in college years, my M400 and I enjoyed popularity in our region of Northern New Jersey. I soon learned the technique to play sustained chords over eight seconds, by lifting each finger momentarily before tape stopped. At the age of 19! I only had one tape frame at the time, and only problems experienced were caused by my own inexperience of key adjustments. A hard-learned lesson after I snapped three tapes!

Being a college copycat band, we never had any original material. Our only surviving recordings of concerts are on 7" 4-track tapes, in former member's basement somewhere in NJ. I did run the M400 through a standard mixer of the era, and reduced the "hot" signal, as not to overdrive the reverbs we were using. I can't recall much more than that. Inverse to Mike Pinder, I chose electronics as career instead of music, realizing my shortcomings in that area.

A marketing arrangement by Dallas Music was "Mellotron Clinics" around the East Cost. I visited three of these, in NY, NJ and Norfolk, VA. Mr. Norman Seldin brought three 400's to demonstrate. It was the first time I heard the M400-SFX tapes! The time frame was 1973-1975.

Finally, among other "firsts," I was one of the first to play the Mark V in spring 1976, at Dallas Arbiter's office in Allendale, NJ. This was 3 months before the collapse, and just before the creation of Sound Sales by Bill Eberline. I had received a photocopy of a hand-drawn block diagram of Mark V wiring in Allendale. Later I discovered this was Les Bradley's own writing!

In 1979, I had dinner at Bill/Nancy Eberline's home in CT, and played the Mark V in his living room. I missed my chance to buy a hardwood M400 cabinet made by a local craftsman, the nice one with the engraved "M" logo on the back. In 1981, I was the first to play the 4-Track Mellotron, in Martian Blue, at the Bomar factory in Southbury CT. Haven't seen it since, but I have the brochure of it.

Because of my 33-year familiarity with the Mellotron, I had in-person contacts with the sellers and distributors of the 'Tron in the USA from day one. I personally befriended Bill Eberline of Sound Sales in Conn. The Mark VI Mellotron sold by Dave Kean is a tribute to his love for the instrument. He has outlived the entire previous era of Mellotron sales and manufacturing in the United States, "first time 'round." Originally, the Mellotron name appeared in 1972 with Dallas Arbiter, and faded away in 1982 with Bomar (4-track manufacturers.). DK has endured 11 years now. I have not seen a Mark VI to precisely critique the machine, so any response I give regarding the instrument is purely conjecture, but it appears to be a marvelous cooperative effort across oceans/continents.

I've owned my original M400, purchased new since July 1973—worked two summers in a dirty warehouse to get it. During my personal Mellotron revival in 1997, I found the M300 in Connecticut, sold by a former member of Sound Sales. In bad shape, I lovingly restored the unit. It originally was Dave Kean's, and seen on his videos. That particular unit was once restored by John Bradley (of Streetly Electronics), and initialed inside as such. I've also acquired a rare Mark I. My fourth instrument, called the JK-MK6, has as its heart two popular M400's, one owned by Felix Pappalardi and the other by ELO. More on those below…

I had been actively pursuing a Mark II for years and years, ever since the "Mellotron Music Console" slipped through my fingers in 1976. This was the SAME machine used by the band Gracious, an SFX-Console with music tapes and dual foot pedals. It was offered for sale from Mellotronics in 1976 for 2,000 Pounds. The band Big-Elf now has that machine.

On to "Julia." I had corresponded with Robert Laughton in California. Through the grapevine, I learned that Mr. Laughton wished to part with his Mark II. In May 1998, it arrived cross-country, sadly only two days after John Bradley returned to the UK from Vermont. Various subtle hints of the machine led me to inquire further of its history. The S/N wasn't 126 as thought, but 124. John Bradley informed me that S/N 124 was on record as NEVER returning for Mark II upgrades. Furthermore, I learned that this particular unit was once owned/played by Gordon Reid of the *Rime* CD. It also was sampled by Nick Magnus, and these samples were used on Marillion CD *Brave*. Gordon Reid and I have remained in contact since, and he has provided me with a letter of provenance—hence the name "Julia," after Gordon's contribution to the Mellotron Album, *The Rime Of The Ancient Sampler*.

So it seems that I have one of three KNOWN Mark I's in existence. There are theoretically seven more out there somewhere. Two others are owned, coincidentally by John Bradley (with "three-arse" bench seat), and Martin Smith (both in the UK). I totally disassembled the Mark I, cabinet and all. Using my woodworking/electronics skills, the cabinet now appears almost new! The restoration work is still in process, but haste is not an issue for me. When completed/assembled/working, I'll have the only Mark I in the USA! – so far.

The saga of the JK-MK6 (so numbered as 6, not VI, as not to cause confusion with Dave Kean's official model) began in 1997. Realizing I could not find or afford a real Mark V, I decided to build a special instrument as a 35th Anniversary tribute model. Dubbed the JK-MK6, I decided upon the name before DK revealed his plans to build his new model, which is based on the M400. The JK-MK6 is based more on the Mark V, and has double keyboards, as Mark-series Mellotrons always had previously. The cabinet is my custom tribute design. It features a strong Mark V presence in front, with controls ahead of the keys. The top sides overlap like the M300, and lower sides feature speaker grilles, as with Mark I/II models. Its dimensions are 95% of the Mark V. The exterior is all exotic veneers, with inlay pattern on edging, front-top-back. Within, two M400's reside, from machines used by Mountain and ELO. Capstans are joined by custom-made coupling, and they look/work like a single Mark V capstan.

The electronics are all my design—new IC pre-amps, active bass/treble control, reverb drivers, and power amps. I'm using my electrical engineering background to give to the Mellotron what it inspired me to do in 1974. The multiple-EQ controls are featured only elsewhere on the 4-Track, which had bass-mid-treble for each of the four tracks. Work is still continuing on the instrument. The good part of this is that my power amp design will be of importance to all Mark I/II owners who are presently missing the original units.

My most memorable (story) was in 1972, when the Moody Blues appeared as part of their "Seventh Sojourn" tour. I attended Madison Square Garden in NYC, and was captivated by Mike Pinder's use of the 'Tron. He played a rare 15-minute rendition of the "Voyage" that enthralled the entire audience! I found myself near stage exit after the concert and had the chance to personally shake Mike Pinder's hand. Immediately afterwards, I set about to work hard and save money to buy my own Mellotron.

I also attended every Yes/Genesis concert in NYC from 1972-1977. I saw countless local bands in the region use the 'Tron during the 1970's, but never saw any problems encountered. The most unusual gig seen was in a bar, attached to bowling alley. I conversed with the keyboardist, who said he wished to get Mellotron tapes recorded with female voices—this in 1976.

Ken Leonard (owner, M400 #805)

This is the quick story of my 805:

Kurdt Vanderhoof, who lives in Washington State, was in need of cash to purchase a vintage "clear" (see-through) Ludwig drum set (c. 1976), and he decided to get rid of one of his two M400s. He posted it to the Mellotronists list, and I jumped in at the right time to bid for the beastie (after he'd lowered the price enough), and he shipped it to my house. I had never seen one before, so when it arrived I had a look-see inside. The bloody thing was nearly empty! Sure, there was some stuff in it, but it was mostly air. Did I get ripped off on an Internet deal? What the hell?

I poked around some more and began to take inventory. Tapes, frame, motor, motor controller (oops, cable fell off, gotta snap it back on), keys, capstan, switch, knob, cables...I guess that was it. So I plugged it in. The AC cable was a frazzled mess, like most of them. Try getting the funky connector on the back of a 'Tron power supply! I turned the switch, and nothing. No whirring, nothing. So I shut it off and waited a few minutes and went back to it. Second time was the charm. I guess this thing had a ghost in it that went away, and it spun up without a hitch. Through an old mixer and some 'phones I got my first taste of an in-the-flesh Mellotron: a flat-sounding, out-of-tune, noisy flute. Perfect!

It's been working fairly fine ever since. I've adjusted the keyboard I don't know how many times. Anyone will tell you that you do indeed get Mellotronists' Hunchback doing that; it can be an hours-long operation adjusting the pinch roller and the pressure pad on 35 keys. I've threaded up a new frame with tapes, and that took a while, too. It was a set of tapes I got from Dave Kean, and toward the end he'd written me a note on the tape that he knew I'd find well into my threading ordeal: "Hi Ken! Having fun?" Ha! Hell, he's threaded millions of these things, so he knows.

When I tell most people that I have a Mellotron, they stare at me blankly or just say, "A what?" Then I have to explain. Shortly after 805 came in, I started dating a young lady who was fascinated with what I told her about the machine. "I've got to see it—it sounds neat!" Hey, my kind of girl! She came over to check out 805, and I'd left the panels off for her to see the tapes going up and down in the frame as I played some of my usual drek. She laid down on the floor behind the machine and watched the tapes, content to stay there and just listen to what I was playing and watching the machine work. Talk about the right woman!

The right woman, that is, until she made a recommendation. "Ya know, Ken, I think 805 would look good painted in a pastel color with a seashell motif." It was not long after that this girl and I parted company. 805 is still around, though. White with black feet, no seashells.

Fortunately, 805 was in good shape when he arrived almost two years ago (April 1998). I had to do a low noise modification in the power supply (with instructions from Dave Kean), but all that took was some soldering. Aside from that he's in good shape, perhaps a bit dinged around the corners and in need of a good paint job.

I've had my share of interesting 'Tron 911 calls. Here are a few, in no particular order:

1) Muffler man.
"Ken, I just took delivery of a 'Tron, but the sound coming out is really muffled. Help!" I grabbed my usual set of tools (socket for the nylock nuts on

the keys, regular screwdriver, alcohol (for cleaning stuff), emery cloth, and a demagnetizer and headed out to Newton, MA, where the emergency was.

Problem 1: The amp was plugged into the volume control jack. "I get nothing when it's plugged into the back, just here." A wee bit of cleaning up cured that.

Problem 2: So we'd gotten sound out the proper jack, but it was still massively muffled. I was quite perplexed, but then I looked into the top of the machine again and busted out laughing. "Who tossed these tapes in here?" I asked. The new owner answered, "The guy who sold it to me." I let this new owner know that the light brown side is where the sounds are recorded, and it should not be visible from the top...Yep, the tapes were put in upside down. No, he wasn't looking forward to reinstalling all the tapes, but I showed him the basics, and he said he'd take it from there. Last I heard his 'Tron was pretty happy and no longer quite so muffled!

2) Being in the 20th percentile.

Once a CMC-10 controller starts to go bad, there's nothing you can do to make your Mellotron happy. It always sounds like a sick dog. So you shoot the controller and replace it. So this 'Tron owner rang up Mr. Dave Kean, who sent out his last SMS-5 motor controller. Yours truly got the phone call to wire this up, so I grabbed my desoldering/soldering station (and my other tools), and off I went.

We got the old controller out and put in the new one. That was the easy part. I then spent a few hours moving wires around on the power supply. The type of connector they use on the power supply uses a plug with several wires on it. To attach wires to this plug, you push the wires into some pins (short, thin tubes with rounded ends) then somehow solder them inside there. Now THAT was a bitch. I had to crank my soldering iron way up, find a way to hold this plug with all these pins in place, get the solder heated up enough to melt, then pull the old wire out. After that I had to get the new wire, stick it into the plug, and somehow heat up the solder again so that wire would stay where I put it. A few burned fingers and a few hours later, I finally got things in place. Whew!

We put the power supply back into the M400, snapped on the power switch, and nothing. We checked and double-checked the power supply and the wiring job we did, and it was all to spec. A quick call to Dave Kean had his diagnosis: "Oh, is this particular wire in this location?" "Yep." "OK, well that explains it. You have one of 'those' power supplies. Some 'Trons have a power supply that is slightly different, and you've got the one that was in about 20 percent of the 'trons I've seen." Nice—we're in a minority. Dave relayed a new set of instructions, and I went back to the soldering iron and reworked everything. After checking and double-checking my work, we loaded the power supply into the 'Tron, cabled it all up, and it purred to life. Whew!

3) Shielding?

We don't need no steeeenkin' shielding! Someone was due to take delivery on a Mark II, newly refurbished by Streetly. What a beautiful machine it was, too. We let it acclimate for a little while (get used to the temperature and humidity of its new home while we went out for stouts and lunch), then we were ready to fire it up. The owner called Martin Smith to have him walk us through a checklist before turning it on (Lord only knows what happens to those things during shipping). So we had Martin on the cordless phone while we walked around the Mark II looking at this and poking at that.

Things looked great, so it was time to turn it on. I was behind the machine, and I watched the voltage meter on the power supply fire right up, and the box came to life. We heard the thud in the speaker as the amps kicked in.

From the right speaker we got this bizarre beeping sound for a second. But then it went away. OK, back to business. Martin walked us through cycling the stations, and then we were ready to play the machine. It sounded just great! I was congratulating Martin on a job well done, when we heard the beep again.

"Oh no. What'n'ell was wrong with the damn thing?"

"Martin, listen to this thing!"

We put the phone near the speaker.

Beeeeeeep beeeeeep...

"Wow, that's odd," he said.

"Yeah, we've got no idea."

"Wait! Are you guys on a cordless phone?"

We all busted out laughing. Yep, the cordless phone's signal was getting into the amp somehow and coming out as a beep. The Mark II was just fine. In fact, John Bradley did a great job on it, just a great machine!

4) Sticky tape.
Another 'Tron owner took delivery of some brand new tapes from Martin in the UK. Seems his tapes come in two flavors: the "piss yellow" stuff or the "pink" stuff. This 'Tron owner wired up some of the pink stuff, and tossed the frame into one of his machines. Well, this pink stuff just doesn't have enough bend to it, so it was often found jammed in the tape take up box.

Loops of it would be flopping around above the capstan, and no amount of yanking on the tape would free it. You had to remove the lid and the keyboard, then the tape would snap back. The owner brought his frame over to my place to try the tapes in 805. I played them for a while, and he played them for a while. Absolutely no jam—none.

Always one for customer service, Martin replaced the pink stuff with the piss yellow stuff. Sure enough, even this stock decided that this particular machine belonging to my friend wasn't where it wanted to be, so the piss yellow stock was summarily crunched (although not as often as the pink stuff). Third time's a charm. Martin provided some different stock (a dark gray or black, if I remember correctly), and those tapes have been fine. Dave Kean provides his tapes on Ampex 456 stock, and I've had only one crunch, and that was while I was messing about adjusting the keyboard. The same tape has been fine ever since. And it's recommended that if a tape gets a bend or crease in it, just grab your favorite iron and put it on low and iron out the crease. So, yeah, these things will eat tapes on occasion. Unfortunately it's an expensive proposition if you do lose a tape. Sigh.

5) Screeching cable rot.
Imagine playing your 'Tron for a while only to be accosted with an absolutely terrible screech in your headphones. I'm talking deafening! You later discover that wiggling the cable going to your preamp deadens the screech. And shortly after playing your tapes again, you discover your tapes have been muffled or even erased!

In their effort to cut costs (or in some bout with poor judgment), Streetly went with the cheapest braided copper cables possible for connecting the major portions of the M400: head block to pre-amp, out of the power supply area (where the pre-amp sends its audio signal) to the volume control jack, then from the volume control jack to the output at the back of the machine. Over time, oxidation destroys the wiring, and any movement (such as switching tracks, which moves the head block) causes the metal in the wires to turn to dust and fail.

Result: Scrreeeeeech!

And in the most unlucky cases when the cable from the head block to the pre-amp fails, it's possible to charge the heads. The next time the tapes flow over the heads, their magnetic content will be screwed, erasing or dulling the sound on the tapes. At $250 a set, that gets expensive. The solution to the screech is replacing the cables and connectors with some good stuff.

Whenever I work on a 'Tron and it involves messing about with the pre-amp or other major electronic component, out comes the demagnetizer. Yes, there are ways to shield the head block from becoming charged (putting a 40K Ohm resistor across the head block cable or shorting out the pre-amp inputs with a screwdriver before plugging in the head block), but why take chances?

I have a TEAC E-3 demagnetizer. When you plug it in and turn it on (far from the 'Tron, mind you), it buzzes, not unlike an electric razor (it also made my "pastel with shell motif" girlfriend's eyes widen, thinking it was something for her). So on you go demagging the heads: in straight, wave over the head, out straight—35 heads' worth. When you switch off the demagger, your hearing is messed up. All you can hear is a washy, phasey, swooshy sound, and everything you hear is distorted. It's amazing what the buzzing of that tool will do to your sense of hearing. At that point you go grab a good stout and wait for your ears to calm down before listening to your 'Tron. I think that should be the final instruction in demagnetizing your 'Tron.

6) Mellotron-related Diseases:

Mellotronist's Hunchback: A spinal condition developed during extensive sessions adjusting the keyboard on a Mellotron (key pressure pads and pinch rollers). Symptoms are a stiff, hunched back. Cure involves stout.

Wobblies: The unintentional variation in speed as a Mellotron plays a tape. Results in an uneven sound. Cure involves getting Mellotronist's Hunchback.

Wedgie: When the played tape will not come out of the take-up box. Symptoms are usually a stuck tape with a series of fan-folds at the entrance slit of the take-up box. Cure: Remove keyboard, let the wedgie fall. If the tape is creased, you may have to iron it. If the tapes continue to jam, move from the "pink" stuff to the "piss yellow" stuff and finally the dark stuff.

Spaghetti: A major failure in a Mark II whose station-changing mechanism has gone nuts. Symptoms include a mass of tangled Mellotron tapes (usually 35 or—in the worst cases—70 of them). Cure: Not even massive amounts of stout will touch this one...

Strangulation: Applies to the sound of a Mellotron tape as it runs out. When tapes run out, they are halted, and it results in a strangulation-type sound, especially with the choirs.

Stiction: The hesitation of a tape to return. Generally you don't know this has happened unless you have the front panel off your machine and observe the tape shuttle halfway up the column. Symptoms include a very short note duration and strangulation the next time you play the note. Cure involves reaching in and grabbing the tape, playing the one next to it, or bouncing the tape (tapping the key until the tape falls), or spreading the pins in the tape frame to give the tape a smidge more room to fall in the column. Usually happens on the most important chord in your song while in the middle of a major concert or during a very expensive recording session.

Zip: The sound a 1/4" tape makes in a Mellotron frame upon return, if you've decided to make your own 'Tron tapes on a 1/4" 2-track deck. Review Einstein's theories on light speed.

Warpage: What happens to a key on a Mark II if it's not used to your climate. Keys can bend so badly they rub against other keys and can't really be played. Cure: John B. in the UK has an apparatus to straighten out a warped key. While the key is away being repaired, your Mark II reminds you of Alfred E. Newman.

Recording with a Mellotron

The Mark II with which I am familiar sounds wonderful out its ancient amps and ancient Wharfdale speakers. Despite line outs (installed by John Bradley of Streetly), the owner of this Mellotron has decided he'll just put a microphone at either of its speakers. It really has that "'tronny" sound, and he wants to capture it. I feel that taking the line outs would lose that "sound," so I'm with him on this one. The M400 requires an external amp. I plug mine right into a mixer and record it from there. In addition to some AC hum (just try to get rid of that from analog gear of any kind), you'll get some noise and other artifacts. To add to the fun, you need to watch the levels closely, since playing too many notes at once may push you over into clipping.

In addition, a "dry" Mellotron is just that—very dry. Various artists have used all kinds of processing, from Leslies to reverb units. I normally throw a little reverb onto #805 and record it like that. (I have a rack of effects and record to a PC set up with Cakewalk digital audio software and an Event Gina digital audio card, the results of which may be heard on my tunes page on **www.kleonard.com**.)

Playing a Mellotron

Perhaps the most quirky thing about Mellotrons is that each one is different. If Duncan Goddard played his and I played mine, they'd be very easy to tell apart by sound. Put two modern synthesizers side by side, and they'll sound about the same. Being made of wood and having a design that's very sensitive, a Mellotron is more of a living instrument. It is affected by heat, cold, humidity, and even its own mood that day. I've played #805 on a Saturday with wobblies and all kinds of crap going on—essentially unplayable (or at least not worthy of recording). By Sunday, it's fine and is a completely different instrument, with no adjustment on my part.

If you've never played one, you're in for it. I won't say you're in for a "treat" though. Because you are pressing down a long, wide key onto a pinch roller and a pressure pad, a lot of power is required to produce a sound. Most Mellotron keyboards are mushy and inaccurate or stiff and not responsive; the feel just isn't the same as a synth or a piano. I have played one or two Mellotrons with well-adjusted keyboards, and they're nicer than what I've got going with #805, but they're by no means very easy to play.

Mellotronists develop their own styles. You've got an instrument that's touchy, so you need to listen to what you're playing and make adjustments in your style along the way. You might be playing a chord only to have one of the notes start to wobble or drop out. You need to press harder on that one note—but not on the other notes you're holding. And sometimes tapes don't return all the way, meaning a certain note may have a shorter life than others, so you need to lift that finger and possibly re-trigger the note (or just forget about it). And, yes, you have about eight seconds, depending on whose set of tapes you have. With the 8-voice choir it sounds like you're strangling some of them when you run out of tape (see "Strangulation" above).

Considering the recordings of the original tapes back in the '60s, the various generations, any clean-ups, transfers to computers, and the adjustment of the machine that cut tapes for your 'Tron, the tapes themselves put in a great many artifacts. Sometimes you have a breathy flute note, but elsewhere on your keyboard will be one that's not so breathy. Add in the adjustment of the pressure pad, and you've got 35 notes that sound different in quality up and down the keyboard. I don't need perfect pitch, since I can tell when you're hitting the low F on 805 because of the way the sound is muffled and sounds like it's straining to come out. Chords can be a nightmare, especially on full-sounding Mellotron tapes, like the 3-violins or the string sections. If you hold down too many notes to make a chord, your sound will become distorted. So you need to lay off. Then of course there's the thud in the high E-flat in the Cello tape set (as well as the tape set combinations that use Cello), as well as my B-flat in the second octave of the 3-violins sound that's so badly distorted it's almost unusable. These are the fault of the source tapes, most likely. Very 'Tron-like.

Faking a Mellotron with Samplers

Sampled Mellotrons are always a touchy subject with me. For me playing a Mellotron is challenging because of what the instrument is. It's imperfect, and you need to play along with it the way it wants to be played, like walking a husky that has a mind of its own. When you press a key on a Mellotron, you'll get a slightly different sound each time. That's part of the beauty of it. These days with modern samplers it seems that everyone is playing a Mellotron on a record, yet very few real 'Trons are in any of the studios. Every note that comes out is the same, and you can tell artists who use the same samples. What's worse is that some artists stretch the Mellotron above its usable range, making for some awful sounding noise. In fact, there's one CD I can't listen to because the artist decided to do this. Perhaps he's not aware of the 35-note limit. Well, he went at least another octave, turning the beautiful Mellotron flute into an awful sine wave.

I feel that all those sample users out there cheapen the Mellotron a little, but there are a few artists, such as Redshift, who do such a great job with the Mellotron sounds in the context of the song that I don't really care. Thankfully those with the real thing (such as Klaus Hoffmann-Hoock [Cosmic Hoffman, RAMP]) are using it. Those without (like Stephen Parsick) borrow his. Others use samples (Redshift, Free System Projekt, the Cure, and many others). So I'm torn on the topic. One part of me loves to hear the sound, but the other wants the sound to be produced from the real instrument. To that end I have offered the services of #805 to my electronic music friends free of charge, but not free of wobblies.

I'm just very glad that the Mellotron is making a bit of a comeback, and loads of people seem curious about it and wanting to use it in recordings. Even my 805 has been used in Michael Oliver and Go, Dog, Go!'s latest album *Pop and Circumstances*. (See my Home Page off **www.kleonard.com**, scroll down in the black box, and you'll see info about that, with sound samples.)

Paul Hoaglin (owner, Mark II #139)

I first became aware of the Mellotron as a wee lad, reading my parents' *Guitar Player* magazines and seeing the ads for *Keyboard* magazine that had pictures of a model 400 in them. I managed to piece it together that this was the famous Mellotron I had read about in some of the articles. Oddly enough, I had heard plenty of 'Tron but didn't know it yet (Beatles, Stones, etc.). It wasn't until I discovered Yes that I was able to identify what I heard as the sound I'd read about, and I was definitely fascinated by it already. However, it was when I experienced a huge upsurge in interest in psychedelic music from '66 to '69 that I realized how much Mellotron there was on the music of the time, and I determined that I was going to make those sounds a part of my musical arsenal someday.

I was still confused as to when the Mellotron became available, though, as I was only aware of the 400 model, and had read that it had only came out in 1970. The big revelation came for me when I read a book called *Rock Hardware*, which chronicled in some detail the history of the Mellotron and mentioned the Bradley brothers by name. This is where I first learned that the Mellotron I had heard on records prior to 1970 was (mostly) the Mark II model, and this is also where I learned that the instrument had two keyboards side by side, and that each keyboard had 18 sounds. Immediately I realized that this was the Mellotron to have, both in terms of its increased number of sounds available, as well as the fact that most of the sounds that had knocked me out the most on records had been done on the Mark II.

Following up on this, I found the mailing address for Streetly Electronics in the back of this book, and wrote them a letter, asking if they still made the Mark II model, or if one was still available. I received phone calls subsequently from both Norman and Leslie Bradley, telling me that they had two Mark II units in storage, and that they needed to sell them as they were in the process of liquidation. I was very young at the time—15 when I first heard from them—and so I wheedled and cajoled my mother, explaining how rare the opportunity was to find one of these instruments, and she eventually gave in and borrowed out of my grandmother's savings. However, between the negotiations and the Bradleys' financial difficulties, it took about two years before the Mark II was ready to ship, and then the shipping itself took several months, as it went by boat. However, in October of 1988, my Mellotron Mark II finally made it out of customs in Oakland, and I brought it home. Unfortunately, between when Leslie and his son John packed it up and when I powered it up, the cycling had failed, so I had to wait while Leslie sent me the clutch spanner so I could manually move the tapes from station to station. The cycling's been out to this very day. (Interestingly, the second Mark II Leslie had when I wrote him eventually ended up as John Bradley's personal instrument.)

Over time I've learned to play the Mellotron very differently than other keyboards, and also very differently for each different sound. To play block chords with the 3 Violins and sound well, it's important to start the next chord before releasing the previous one, or it can sound very abrupt, even with reverb. Often using two hands is necessary even for relatively simple chord changes for that reason, and also to maintain sufficient pressure on the keys to make the tapes contact the heads firmly. Also, on the stock Mark II tapes, the lowest half-octave of flute notes are very, very quiet, and so they often require special attention as regards the signal-to-noise ratio. I do try to use as many of the original Mark II sounds as possible, as I find that many times the "mystery sounds" I've been puzzling out for many years are a combination or unusual usage of the less commonly used Mark II sounds, such as the various organs, mandolins, vibes, accordions, etc.

For recording, I have tried both going direct and running it through an amp, and each option has its own advantages. The best results I've had recording the 3 Violins were running it direct into a V72 valve (tube) pre-amp, though a valve compressor, and then to tape. However, it's important to notch out the hum from the motor for the quieter sounds like the flute, the vibes and the "Harpsichord Effect." Running through an amp can be very good, particularly for the darker sounds like the various brass sounds. An amp can also clean up the sound a bit, especially if the amp's frequency response doesn't really reproduce frequency of the hum and/or the tape hiss. The EQ I use on it depends again on the sound being recorded, but generally I try to get rid of some of the abrasive stuff in the 4 to 5K range. This can help make the violins come out more "transparent" and smooth, especially with a dash of compression. I've never really run effects on it, as the output impedance doesn't really work well with most guitar effects, but I always try to use a volume pedal, rather than the built-in swell pedal, which is quite dodgy and hard to operate. As mine came to me without the internal speakers, I've never had the opportunity to record it that way.

I've only ever owned the one Mark II, but I used a 400 on a recording project on one occasion, and fell in love with the cello sound. In general, the 400 seems cleaner sounding, both from that experience and from close listenings to the available recordings. How much of this is due to the impedance difference in the heads, or the tube versus solid-state pre-amps, or the different EQ on each instrument's master tapes, I can't begin to speculate. I haven't seen or heard the new Mark VI, but I am in favor of new models being built, so I applaud Dave Kean's efforts. I've only had my Mark II at a gig once (and I wasn't the one playing it), and it worked as well as was expected, considering the limitation of no cycling. The funny part of the event was when the house music came on between bands, and people climbed on stage to dance, and several people tried to put their beers on top of it! I panicked, and ran up on stage and told them to get their beers off of my precious instrument! I had to do that a number of times during the course of the evening, but at least I managed to avert disaster. I do, however, entertain plans to gig it again once I get the cycling sorted out and, of course, when the appropriate band comes along. I have a whole system planned for dealing with transporting and maintaining it when that opportunity comes along.

One interesting non-gig-related story that fits the bill, however, is the time that I rented it to Romy, the keyboardist from the group the Wallflowers. I helped lug it for he and the guys he was doing this particular session for, and then went home. Sure enough, when I got home, he'd left a message saying it wasn't working. Apparently, it chose that moment to have the wires that bring power into the pre-amp develop a loose connection, which I'd never encountered before! So I jumped back on a train to San Francisco and went to the studio and puzzled it out for them. A related experience that predated this was when it was residing between sessions at Coast Recorders, also in SF, when the Counting Crows came in for a session. Apparently they were hot to try it out, but the assistant engineer wasn't one of the ones I had shown how to use it, and so between them, they managed to tangle up two tapes on the left-hand keyboard! (To this day I still don't know how—I've never done anything like it myself!) I managed to sort it out and spent a couple of mornings retrieving the tapes and reinstalling them, and after a while, they flattened out fairly well and were not too much worse for it.

Norm Leete (owner, M400 #V1514)

I actually heard the Mellotron (and thought it was stunning) long before I knew what it was. "Strawberry Fields" was on of the first tracks that made my ears prick up. The major "aha" happened when I first played one.

I have never seen them (eight-second playability, tape transport reliability) as limitations, it's just the way they are. That's a bit like saying why don't saxes play chords. For long, drifting pieces, there is the Mellotron Ripple (not an ice cream) where chords are arpeggiated to make the rewind times happen at different times. It's even better if you use an echo or delay as well.

On recording the Mellotron:
Flat EQ with a delay. Used to be a Roland Space Echo, but now is a modern digital job set to about 500 ms and 4 repeats.

I have had two M400's, an EMI and a Streetly M400. The EMI was the first 'Tron I ever played (I bought it from the original owner some years later). It was named the Frankentron, as the keyboard and mainframe seemed to be from different machines, so the serial numbers had been removed. The second one was built specially for Barclay James Harvest, and was the only black vinyl M400 made by the factory (1975—serial number V1514).

The Frankentron (Serial Number—unknown) was bought by the previous owner from a music shop in Bristol in 1975. He had new tapes made by Mellotronics as part of the deal. They were String Section, Male choir and Flutes on the frame in the machine and an additional frame with Vibes, Female choir and Oboe. I met him in about 1977 and we formed a band that went through several line-ups in the following few years. Starting as a two-man Tangerine Dream derived arrangement, we went on to add three more members (and an additional Mellotron!). We went on to become a three keys and drummer line-up and were definitely weird by then. Dressed as a string quartet (I even got the hang of the bow-tie), our stage act included spraying the audience with cornflakes and an unexpected appearance of Sooty (well known English glove-puppet) who was gaffe-taped to the front of the M400, ready for instant deployment!

In the end, the band split, my last gig was playing at the Marquee in London, but we kept in touch and I finally persuaded him to part with the EMI M400 in the early '80s. He saw the Mellotron after being restored and was knocked out by the difference in the machine. The last time I saw it was when I had the chance to lend it to the Strawbs to do their VH-1 broadcast on the lead-up to the anniversary gig (I was there as well—and my tape frames were in the two M400's there that night). To see one of my favorite Mellotron tracks of all time ("Grave New World") being performed live on my M400 was a fitting last act for it. When the band found out I was lending it to them for nothing, as I was a fan, they treated me like a long-lost friend. I don't know who has it now, but it was sold on so that I could get my current M400.

The Frankentron was in a bit of a state, with chunks of veneer missing from the top and sides. Internally, things were even worse. Being an EMI M400, it was manufactured by EMI from kits of parts. Some of the components were not as good as those used on the Streetly machines, and they were not assembled with the tender loving care applied by the Bradleys at the original Streetly factory. As a result, it seems my machine had never functioned as well as it could have.

Some of the problems included old motor control board, sub-standard power supply, and the mechanics out of square. This misalignment meant that the tapes dragged on the guides so the pinch wheels had been adjusted to increase the pressure on the capstan, and still some tapes would drag. In some cases, this was so bad they would squeak while playing. With all this drag, the motor control (an early one) was already struggling to keep the rotational speed of the capstan constant so any more than four notes and the whole instrument would go flat! The motor control took at least 10 minutes to warm up, and made the most awful sound when running (a high-pitched whine).

It was decided, after discussion with Martin Smith and John Bradley of Streetly Electronics, that the cure for all these ills was a complete rebuild. The machine was first stripped down to its component parts. The wooden outer shell was then sent to a car body repair shop where all the dents were filled, edges were made good, and the whole thing rubbed down and primed. The prepared case was then sprayed gloss white using a two-part epoxy finish (not the sort of thing you can do at home).

Meanwhile, the old power supply was rewired. The old CMC10 servo board was also removed and replaced with an SMS board. The inner chassis was then cleaned and made square, ready for re-assembly. Originally, the whole inner chassis was out of square, which meant all the pads and rollers were bent to make them line up, a recipe for erratic pitch and inconsistent behaviour between tape frames. To say that re-assembly is the reverse of disassembly is a bit of an understatement, as a Mellotron has to be put together very carefully for it to work properly (remember that most people's perception that the Mellotron is an awful, unreliable, out-of-tune piece of junk is based on playing un-maintained, or even worse, horribly botched machines).

So the machine was now re-assembled back into its newly re-sprayed case, along with a new power supply, a new motor control card, and the keyboard action was adjusted correctly to give an action much closer to an organ, and not like some sort of perverse exercise equipment. The keyboard action is a modification first tried by Pierre Veilleux and involves moving the position of some of the pivot points and changing the layout of the rear tape guide.

When my machine was delivered back, I could not believe how different it was. It looked new and played unlike any other Mellotron I had ever played. Other observations included: no whine, as the SMS2 is a true servo and not based on PWM switching; no warm up, as the SMS2 doesn't need it; tape frame changing was much easier; and the range (tone) control now has an effect on the sound as the bandwidth is greater (more bass and treble). This meant that the 'string section' that I use extensively had some real bite, and the choir was the best I have ever heard it. Conclusion: not a cheap exercise, but worth every penny.

The Mellotron I currently own (Serial No. V1514) is also of interest as it is the only surviving vinyl (tolex) covered M400 built by Streetly. According to John (Bradley), it was built in 1975 as an experiment, along with a red one. The black one then carried on to be supplied as a special to Barclay James Harvest and was used by them for the next four or five years. I am trying to find independent evidence to support this.

The differences in detail are...

The shape: To allow the vinyl covering to be applied the cabinet is a different shape. The angles at either end that follow the shape of the lid have been straightened out to make covering easier.

The PSU: Has a standard IEC connector avoiding that panic when you cannot find the normal mains lead with the Bulgin connector has gone missing! It also has an SMS2, which improves the overall stability.

The Cabinet is heavier duty than normal. It seems that the idea was to build a tougher version more suited to the conditions found when gigging an instrument. There are two carrying handles on the back (holes in the cabinet) that make lifting far easier. The stability of the cabinet has a secondary effect, as this seems to be one of the most stable M400's I have ever come across. For this reason alone I will not be parted from it.

The plate on the rear states that it was made by Bradmatic. This was the company name that the Bradley Bros. used before Streetly and was reserved for one-off projects that they did from time to time. Internally, there is evidence of the machine being regularly being sent back to Streetly for servicing—so here we have an M400 with a service record!

As for the new Mark-VI, having only seen photographs, what I have seen is not that good. For example, the heads are soldered into a PCB. I recently had the azimuth of my head block adjusted—this would be impossible on the new one. It makes me feel that the idea is a good one (that is, making a new version of the instrument), but has been spoilt by lack of attention to detail and knowledge of how the current instruments work. I hope that sounds fair.

Gary Hahlbeck (owner M400 #167, Mark VI #04, Chamberlin M1 #106)

From the very first time I heard the Moodies *Threshold of a Dream* album, the first Moodies album I was aware of, I wondered a lot about that strange keyboard sound that sounded like a violin section. I was nineteen in 1970, and went to see the Moodies play a concert in the Milwaukee Auditorium. I remember seeing this weird walnut cab that looked a bit like a big fat Hammond, along with a matching speaker cab that seemed to have a whole lot of small speakers in it. So this is what a Mellotron is!

The Moodies started the night with "Gypsy" which was from what was at that time their new album, *To Our Children's Children's Children*. You might know that there are eight bars in the intro before Mike Pinder first plays the 'Tron. That seemed like an eternity to me, I was so hyped to hear if that keyboard sounded as wonderful live as it did on the record. After what seemed like an eternity (an eight bar eternity), the 'Tron was finally played. I knew from that moment on, I had to have a Mellotron. King Crimson further reinforced that belief after I discovered them later that year.

In my day job, I own Sonic Loudspeaker Systems, Inc., as I did in 1970 as well. We sell to about 1,500 music stores nationally, so I frequent music stores and see their new inventory. A year or so later, I saw this really ugly white keyboard at West Allis Music Store in Wisconsin. I asked the combo manager about it and to my amazement, he told me it was a Mellotron. As the keyboard was pre-sold to a guy named Louie Fragassi, he was not too anxious to allow me to play it. Quite frankly, the thing scared him that it might break before delivery. I persisted in my begging, and he relented—for two minutes. Three violins, flutes, and choir. Tiny keyboard, much shorter than I had imagined. Hearing it, again, I knew I had to have one.

By this time I was dating my soon-to-become bride. Every Christmas she would ask me, "What do you want for Christmas?" The standard answer, for almost 30 years, was a Mellotron.

Once in 1983, I almost bought a used 'Tron from B Sharp Music in Minneapolis while on a sales tour for Sonic. The owner of the store hated the thing. He told me he thought it sounded like a "cat that just had its tail stepped on." I offered him $300 for the 'Tron, which he immediately accepted. Several minutes later, he backed out of the deal, and for some reason, refused to sell the thing for any money. In the meantime, I bought every string machine, sample disc, sampler module, and CD-ROM that offered Mellotron sounds. All of these gizmos fell short of the mark.

In the mid '90s, I started a second business servicing and restoring old Vox guitar amplifiers. You can see this business if you like on the net at **ww.voxshowroom.com/northcoast**. One day I received a phone call from a guy that needed a Vox amp repaired. His name was Louie Fragassi. He was the keyboard player for the 1910 Fruitgum Company. I stopped by his place to drop off an AC-50 head I had just repaired for him. Sitting in the middle of his practice room was a broken down M400 Mellotron, serial #167. Incredibly, this was the same Mellotron I had seen 25 years earlier at West Allis Music Center. A bit of coaxing and $900 later, #167 moved to my house, with my wife wishing me "Merry Christmas" over and over for the 25 years I had begged her for a 'Tron.

While doing a restoration on this 'Tron, I met Dave Kean. Dave and I became friends, and one night over beers and a Mexican dinner in North

Hollywood, he asked me about making the cabinets, spill boxes, and pinch rollers for what eventually became the Mark VI 'Tron. My old #167 became the model to work from, and about a year later the very first Mellotron Mark VI was shipped to Oasis. My love for the instrument turned into actually participating in the manufacture of the new 'Trons.

I have recently taken delivery of my Mark VI. It is a wonderful machine. The tube pre-amp gives a bit more of that Mark II sound to the unit, and the half-speed function is very cool. The retraction of the tapes is greatly improved, an area that was always a bit of a sticking point on #167. There is an extra set of 35 rollers to aid in lessening the friction while rewinding. If the new instrument has a flaw, I haven't found it yet.

Just for the record, I now also own a mint Chamberlin M1.

Ken Merbler (owner, Mk II #247, M400 #1001 & #1217)

I first heard the Mellotron sound when I started listening to the Moody Blues. I loved the violin-type sound and the other sounds they were getting. It seemed unique to them; no other band I heard had that same sound. It was kind of a lonely, haunting sound. I later learned that this was the Mellotron, a rare English keyboard instrument that they had somehow acquired. That was my "aha" moment – "aha, that's what that sound is!" I think I read about it on the cover of *In Search of the Lost Chord*. Even though I played the guitar and not a lick of keyboard, I loved the sound of that Mellotron more than any other instrument. We had a local garage band, and we played parties and dances, but we never had a keyboard player. I always dreamed of having a Mellotron in our band, but the rest of the guys were into hard rock, and even a keyboard player would not have been accepted. So, we just played our Led Zeppelin and Aerosmith covers, with the occasional David Bowie tune thrown in.

My very first rock concert was the Moody Blues, back in 1971, in Orlando, Florida at the Orlando Sports Stadium. I remember seeing Mike Pinder from my seat toward the back of the bleachers. I can still remember him playing the Mark II. All I knew at that time was that it looked like an Organ, but it didn't sound like one. When he played "The Voyage" and "Have You Heard", there was a white spotlight on him (this was his solo) as he played and talked "when the white eagle of the north is flying overhead. . ." and then he made that Mellotron growl (I later learned he was turning the pitch control and stomping the volume pedal), and it rattled the entire stadium hall. I remember thinking, man, he's going to blow that thing up!

I remember that I started listening to the Moodies around 1970-1971, so all of their albums were new to me, even though some had been recorded years earlier. There was a progressive rock station, WORJ, in an orange grove in central Florida, which played what they called "progressive rock," including many Moody Blues tunes. I used to get very excited when I heard a new one, then I would rush out and buy the newly discovered album. I always thought it would be great to actually have a Mellotron, but never dreamed I could own one because they were so scarce—I had never seen one, outside of the Moody Blues concert. To this day, the Moodies are the only band I have ever seen use one in concert (a Mark II).

I later discovered that there were other bands who used the Mellotron, Genesis being the main one. But for me, nobody put it all together as well as the Moody Blues.

Soon I started college and put away the musical toys. After that, the career came first. It wasn't until more than years later that I discovered (on the web) that I could actually purchase a Mellotron. I read all about them on Dave Kean's web site and started to think about buying one.

When I bought my first Mellotron, two years ago, I had never played keyboards. But that didn't stop me. Around the same time, I purchased a small MIDI controller keyboard. This was easy to play compared to the Mellotron. When I started playing the Mellotron, I noticed that I had to keep even pressure on the keys, had to stop at eight seconds, and had to put up with out of tune notes and wobblies. The Mellotron requires a lot of adjusting, and that takes some getting used to. As for the eight-second limit, it was hard at first, but now it's second nature. I find the Mellotron much easier to record with than to play live, because you can record in short intervals and splice everything together, after multiple takes. It takes a really good keyboardist to play complete songs on a Mellotron. The reliability issue is with me every day. Often I prefer to use one M400 over the other, because one will be out of tune and instead of fixing it, I'll just use the other one.

I like to use plenty of reverb, especially on the 3-violin sounds. That's almost as important as the sound of the Mellotron itself. Sometimes the 3-violin sound can be high-pitched and harsh, so when I hear that, I'll try to knock some of the high pitched unpleasant tones off using the EQ. I don't use any other effects on the Mellotron. It sounds beautiful as it is, with a good bit of reverb thrown in.

I own three Mellotrons. The first one, M400 #1217, was owned by Cinderella recording studio in Nashville, Tennessee. I discovered this Mellotron through an ad in *Vintage Guitar* magazine. The owner, Wayne Moss, was in a "Country Acid" band in the 1970s called Barefoot Jerry. They recorded several albums, and #1217 was featured on one of the cuts, "Cade's Cove," along with a Minimoog. The owner swore that the tape frame once belonged to John Lennon, and gave me a "Certificate of Authenticity" stating this fact. He claimed that one of the Mellotron reps came to their studio one day and tried to help them adjust #1217 to get it to sound right. The Mellotron rep told them that he would adjust the settings and replace the pinch rollers, and if that didn't take care of the problem, he would replace the tapes with John Lennon's very own set, which he happened to have with him. Well, he ended up replacing the tape set, and that's the one I have now. Once in a while you may hear Ken Leonard or I jokingly refer to it as the "John Lennon" tape set. Martin (Smith of Streetly Electronics) doesn't think that it's true, but that tape set is one of the original "BBS" tape sets, and it sounds and works better than any tape set I have. Each tape has "BBS" written on it. It is the standard 3-violin, flutes and cellos set.

I wanted a Mellotron so badly that I ended up with two identical machines. About six months before I found #1217, I had contacted Martin to see if he could restore an M400 for me. He said that they would try to find one to restore, but I couldn't wait, so I bought #1217 when I saw the ad. A couple of days after this, Martin told me that they had found an M400 for me, so I agreed to buy this one also (I had given him my word and I didn't want to back out of the deal). So, that's how I came to acquire M400 #1001, the rebuilt Streetly unit. I rationalized this by saying that, "Well, if one Mellotron is broken I can always use the other one." Actually, the way it works out, it's more like, "There's always a Mellotron that needs to be worked on."

The Mark II (#247) came about because I could afford it, and it was the one thing in the world I really wanted at the time. There were so few of them made, and they are so desirable, that I know I won't lose money on it, so there's really no reason not to own it, financially. I don't regret that decision, even though I have had some maintenance issues with it. I don't expect ever to sell it, and hope to record some beautiful music with it. And, on top of the music, what a conversation piece!

One thing that amazes me when these Mellotrons are shipped is that no matter how much you prepare, you still have to do a lot of last minute scrambling. It was incredible that nothing went wrong on the day it arrived, though plenty could have. I really had to coordinate a lot of things in a short period of time–and this was after preparing for over a year. First of all, the freight company refused to deliver the Mark II to my house. It seemed that they changed their rules since I purchased my M400. I didn't find this out until the Mark II was sitting in the warehouse. I had two options—I could hire an independent "broker" to clear the shipment through customs, and they would arrange to have someone deliver it to my house. The second option was for me to be my own broker, to clear it through customs myself, and to arrange for the shipping myself. I took this option because it gave me more control over the situation, and if I used someone else, it could take a week or so, and I wasn't going to leave the Mark II in a warehouse in Boston for a week.

Unfortunately, by taking this responsibility, I had to take a day off work and drive all over the place. I had to go to the freight company, pick up papers and write them a check, go to U.S. Customs at the airport, give them the papers and write them a check, then go to a warehouse, and give them some more papers. In addition to all this, I had to hire some movers at the last minute. And, of course, I had to pay them cash since they had never dealt with me before. So the movers (three guys in a truck) met me at the warehouse where I directed their truck to an open bay and got a forklift to get the Mark II. That was nerve-wracking, watching that forklift driver swing around the corners with that Mark II flight case. Thank goodness for the case. Then, when the movers got the 'Tron loaded in the truck, they brought it to my house and we got it into my house without much problem. So when I look at my Mark II, I can remember the hell I went through to get it. But it does sound fine. It is a totally different animal than a 400. I have to be careful that I don't gush about it too much, but the sounds are unique and it is indeed a much better instrument than a 400.

I have three M400 tape frames. I will be getting a fourth set of tapes next month. The sounds are: Flutes, 3-Violins, and Cellos (the "Lennon" set); 8-Voice Choir, String Section, and St. John's Wood Church Organ; Mark II Brass, 3-violins, and Vibes; and M300A violins, M300B violins, and Ian McDonald Flutes (coming in May).

In addition, I have 36 sounds on the Mark II with the optional left-hand Lead tape set. The right-hand set is the standard set, the left-hand set includes M300 A & B Violins, Male, Boys, Female Choirs, String Section, Viola, GC3 Brass, Orchestra, Gothic, Woodwinds, Oboe, Bass Accordion (for "Watcher")/ Tubular Bells split, St. John's Wood Church Organ, 8-Voice Choir, Solo Violin, and probably some others I can't think of.

I congratulate Dave Kean for his accomplishment (the Mark VI). I've never heard or played one, so I don't know how they are. I'd like to see one in person. I'd imagine they play at least as well as a "new" M400 would, and he does have some improvements over the originals. I like the SMS5 motor controller board with the dual speed switch. I put one in my M400 #1217 to replace the original CMC-10 motor control board, and it has played beautifully since. It was the best thing I could have done to improve the sound from that unit. It got rid of the audio whine and the hum also, and made the unit stable and greatly reduced the wobbly sound I used to get when putting pressure on they keys.

Because I never gigged with a Mellotron, I don't have any personal stories. I guess one funny story I could tell is the day that Michael Oliver and his friends came over to record some Mellotron tracks for his new album. He had his recording engineer and his bass player with him, and the plan was to record some tracks on Ken Leonard's machine and then come to my house and record on my machine. Ken and I had been anticipating this day for months, and Ken was especially focused on having his M400 well adjusted so that everything went well for the recording session. However, 'Trons being what they are, when Michael started recording his Mellotron licks, Ken L's C3 note sounded very flat. Every time Michael would play this note, we would all look at each other and grimace. It was pretty funny. Eventually, Michael finished his two songs, and did a very professional job. Most of it was done in a single take. Then they came over to my house. Well, my newly restored M400 was having troubles of its own. It sounded OK, but that pink-backed tape was giving me nightmares. It would not snap back after the note was played, so when Michael played on #1001, I had to keep diving down between his legs to return the tapes. But this is what happens with Mellotrons.

After the recording sessions, Ken L. and I agreed that his M400 sounded badly out of tune but Ken L. told me "If you ever mention this, I'll deny it," so I never did (until now). We both figured that Michael Oliver would somehow fix those flat notes in the studio. Well, much to our horror, when we heard the CD those bad notes were (and are) still there for all to hear, so we had very mixed emotions about our involvement in the recording sessions (our names and machines were credited in the CD liner notes). Since then, Ken and I have learned to love the songs, flaws and all, so it doesn't really matter now. But for a while there, we were walking a fine line between being both proud and ashamed at the same time.

There is a funny Michael Pinder story I heard Justin Hayward (I think) tell on a radio talk show one night. It seems that the Moodies were introduced and as they went on stage Michael was playing the opening chords to "Higher and Higher." The whole stage was flooded with smoke and dry ice as the crowd screamed, and the rest of the band took to the stage. Then when the smoke cleared, the music stopped and there was Michael Pinder, standing over his Mellotron with a flashlight. The rest of the band immediately exited the stage, leaving Michael peering into the top of the Mellotron by himself on stage, with the fans still screaming.

I guess this is funny to me, because I know how fragile Mellotrons are. Also, I can put myself in his shoes. When our band used to practice, we would do it very loudly in someone's garage. On several occasions, the police would come. Once, the police came and everyone ran away, and I was left there standing by my amp with my guitar, so I know how Michael must have felt when he was abandoned by his bandmates. At least I didn't have an audience, though.

John K. Beresford (owner, M300 #005, M400 #1398)

I am 38 presently, and in 1967-68 when I was about 6 years old, my elder sister would religiously tape the top 40 on the Alan Freeman Show—BBC Radio 1 on Sunday afternoons on her "state of the art" reel-to-reel. Being so young and having those sorts of parents, I would be packed off to bed where I would drift off to sleep to the sound of the top 40 being played back every night in the bedroom next door until the next Sunday's program. I now have a reasonable knowledge and love of late '60s hits. But the songs I would wait for before I finally drifted off were "Strawberry Fields Forever," "World," "Kites," "Blackberry Way," "Let's Go to San Francisco," "This Wheel's on Fire," etc.

I fell in love with the sound; that gliding mysterious sound, and I remember even at that age trying to figure out what it was. It was definitely keyboard-ish but not an organ, not one of these new synthesizer things. So my love of the 'Tron began at a very early age and well before I knew what I was listening to! Then there was a gap. I was the only kid at junior school into Led Zep (who I saw at Sheffield City Hall in '73 when I was 11!), Deep Purple, etc. Then at secondary school, my history teacher, who was rather more hip than the rest, got a bunch of us into Genesis, Yes, and Barclay James Harvest. This was a complete revelation because suddenly there was that sound again and all over the place, too!

We quickly booked to see Genesis at London's Hammersmith Odeon. I think it was in 1976 (Trick of the Tail tour). I don't know if you have ever heard a recording of any of that tour but never has the trade mark Mellotron-bass pedal-electric 12-string combination been so "in your face." I had never heard the choirs before live, my hair stood on end, the gravitas of the brass at the end of "Supper's Ready" and the violins everywhere tugged at the old heart-strings as they still do today. We left that concert hall physically and emotionally shattered. It really was a revelation. Back at school we still couldn't figure out how this damned Mellotron thing worked. So my mate who was studying design decided to do a project on the thing and wrote off to Streetly. A reply duly came together with drawings a full description and price list. I remember avidly reading this stuff and not believing that this bizarre nutty mechanism could produce the kind of sounds that reduced us to jelly a few weeks before. I was just totally fascinated and hooked and I wanted one! But the prices were something else! I've been a Mellotron nut case ever since, a true enthusiast if there ever was one!

I should say now that I am not what you would call a musician. In fact, I only play guitar really, and badly at that. I don't find the eight-second limit a real problem now, but it's funny how when I turn to the other keyboards, I find myself treating them as if they too have the same thing! As you probably know there is a variety of ways to get around this problem:

—The Mellotron ripple—arpeggiating open chords usually with both hands and with lots of reverb or echo. I don't use this much.

—Moving around the keyboard more to avoid long notes

—When changing between chords that contain a similar note to release that note just before the next chord is engaged. I use this a lot.

—Doing a Wakeman and introducing a single trill to the long note to give it a chance to rewind.

Tape transport reliability doesn't really affect my approach to playing but I religiously clean out and polish all the relevant bits monthly as part of the maintenance routine. Polishing 52 turnbuckles is a bit of a chore, but I love it. Strange!

I used to use a Yamaha digital reverb on my old M400, but my M300 has a superb Hammond spring line on board anyway. You can, on the M300, direct all of the signal through the springline to give a more ethereal effect. Woolly Wolstenholme does this on "Galadriel" and "Mocking Bird."

I own an M400 in white, Streetly refurb, that came from Canada (from Pierre's collection), but was originally a Mellotronics machine. I think the number was 1398, but I need to check that out. Martin tells me this is now with the Charlatans and painted black. M300 #005 came up in the Vemia auction last year, and Martin and I picked it up from a synth shop in Bristol. The story is that it originally was bought for a Cinema somewhere in Wiltshire, southwest England where it entertained the punters between screenings. The Cinema burnt down in the 1970s and in the fire, the LSA300 speaker cabinet was consumed. The 'Tron, however, covered only by its muff, suffered only a slight amount of water damage to the base, and the drive motor which needed replacing. There are higher forces protecting the Mellotron!

I intend this summer to try and find out more about this cinema and if I can find anyone who remembers the 'Tron, even who played it and the fire itself. I have no pics (of my Mellotrons) at present, but a good identical 'Tron is Jerry Korb's, a very good picture which is featured on David Cilia's site: **(http://perso.wanadoo.fr/egrefin/sommaire/mellotro/300jerry.html).**

I have mixed opinions on the Mark VI. It's like making reproductions of antique furniture. I take pride in the fact that I have an example of a rare and classic instrument, and I admit to being a little disappointed that someone was now making reproductions. At the same time I'm sure they are very good and will make the 'Tron more widely available but to me they are not the real thing.

I'm sure Blue Weaver has already told you of the occasion at an open-air gig in the USA where his "baked" 'Tron stretched all its tapes on the very first and opening chord. I've not heard first hand how Woolly coped when his 'Tron went haywire halfway through a major headlining gig at the Rainbow in London—but if you can get that it would be worth it. Woolly is a very entertaining guy and is big friends with Martin Smith.

Personally, I don't have any tales other than the numb, aching feeling I get when I think back to when I was about 18 and we walked into the smallest musical instrument shop in Sheffield. It was a tiny place that only ever dealt in drum kits and guitars, no keys. We opened the door and it banged into something huge taking up the whole floor of the shop in front of the small counter. It was my first encounter with a Mark II Mellotron. This thing was like a sideboard with keys on! The shop owner was going bananas because his partner had bought this thing one day while he was away from the shop not knowing what it was. Now only two people could get into the shop at once. But I was a spotty school kid and he wouldn't let anyone of us look at it, as no one else could get in the shop while we were there. We couldn't afford the £300 he wanted for a quick sale and we certainly couldn't get it home on the bus! We probably couldn't even get it in the house! So we left it and it disappeared. I often wonder if it still is in the area. It could be just at the end of the street. Who knows?

My M300 is presently in Martin's workshop awaiting a full service, and he tells me it is to be done soon, hopefully at the end of April (depending on how it behaves, of course). The tape set on my M300 will be a custom set of Mark II/M400 sounds at both ends of the keyboard with perhaps a couple of Mark II rhythms for novelty.

Mike Dickson (owner, M400 #996)

Obviously I couldn't tell you when I first heard it, since it has been heard (and mistaken) on numerous pop records from the late '60s onwards. The first time I was aware of the "sound" was probably on some early Genesis records, maybe *Nursery Cryme*—the sort of stuff I was buying when I was 13 or so. The first time I heard the sound "with knowledge" was King Crimson's *In the Court of the Crimson King*, which I first heard in 1978 when I was 14. That album entirely changed my view of music in general and in particular. As well as the impossible-sounding 'togetherness' of the band, there was also a sound which was heard most prominently on songs such as "Epitaph" and the title track, the nature of which I knew I had heard before but the substance of which I knew I had never encountered.

Research showed this thing to be a "Mellotron." I had no idea how it worked, what it actually did, or how you played it, but I knew from that point onwards that I had to have one someday. That thought nearly obsessed me for several months and caused me to buy up all the remaining King Crimson albums. I used to dream about them as well, which was a bit odd considering that I didn't know what they looked like. The whole album was like getting my brain rewired, and the impact of the Mellotron was part of the whole, so there was no real "aha" on the individual contribution of the instrument alone. I turned up a lot more references to it here and there (mostly in playing credits from books on rock music) and used to buy albums because they featured a 'Tron somewhere.

If anything, the "aha" happened when I first got the second Pavlov's Dog album, *At the Sound of the Bell*. The intro to the first song simply features voice and Mellotron choir, a sound that I had heard before (again) on albums by the likes of Genesis. This time, though, it was different. Any instrument capable of making that noise was worth spending money on.

I may be lucky, but I have never had any major problems with the instrument, certainly no problems that would require me to think about altering the way I play the keyboard. You get a "feel" for the Mellotron and get to learn the slightly dodgy pad/roller contacts and compensate a bit, but overall it's as straightforward as any other. When gigging, I tend to play with the front cover off, just in case there are any tapes that stick, but I've yet to have any. It also makes for an interesting thing for the punters to watch from the front of the stage.

The limited playback time, though, clearly has an impact on the way the instrument is phrased. Normally, I never stab at chords, tending instead to hold on a triad or cluster and slide the chord a note at a time into the next chord, and so on. That way you get a blurring of the chord as well as pleasing phrase transition. If the chord goes on for a very long time then you can learn to phrase the notes in a chord a second or so apart so that when one tape starts to run out you can drop the key and pick it back up later, moving onto the next note in the sequence. It's not a keyboard you can really play sitting down, as you really have to lean into the keys to give the maximal contact.

I use several techniques, depending on the sort of result I am trying to achieve. I have several favorites:

(1) Record the same track twice on separate takes, each in opposite channels. Since the recorded sounds are "organic," then they are not constant across the entire signal. Hence, minor time and phrasing differences between the channels

gives a 180 degree separation, whereas the basic sound merges across the channels, which taken together gives a very broad spread across the stereo pan.

(2) Play it through a Leslie.

(3) Play it through a very, very tiny speaker indeed and record it with either a high-quality microphone or the cheapest mic that will pick the sound up. (Speakers inside a PC are good for the playback)

(4) Saturated, wet reverb (choir, strings...)

(5) Chorus pedal (brass, flute...)

I normally record it direct, using an Alesis MIDIVerb II as the effect rack, although I have played it through my Hammond's spring line reverb unit. One thing I have absolutely never done is record it digitally—it always seems to lose something. Whether this is down to tape saturation or whatever, I don't know.

I own Mellotron M400 serial number #996. I came by it through my position as the administrator of "Elephant Talk," the King Crimson Internet mailing list. I attended a playback of their *Night Watch* album in London in September 1997, and there I met John Bradley and Martin Smith (of Streetly Electronics) and promptly went on to hog the King Crimson *Red* Mellotron and the Skeletron all afternoon. I had played one before, but never at such an indulgent level! I spoke with Martin at length that day and was fixed on buying one when I left the venue. I just knew that this would be my only chance to get a decent one. I confirmed the deal with Martin a month or so later and received my M400 in January 1998. I took four days off work when I got back just to play with it. I wish I had made it the full week.

I now have three frames:(1) 3-violins/8-voice choir/solo flute, (2) church organ/string section/brass, and (3) Ian MacDonald flute/'Dickson Strings'/cello

The 'Dickson Strings' are a special hybrid that Martin (Smith) put together for me, being 40/60 percent of viola and M300-A strings. It is a uniquely melancholy sound and mixes very well with the cello.

The one story I specifically recall the most was a gig in Dundee I was involved in about a year ago. I was asked to play the 'Tron on a couple of songs for a friend's band, so we lugged it up the east coast of Scotland and the rather steep hills of Dundee to a bar venue, the name of which I escapes me. The place was really busy and incredibly noisy, so much so that the sound of the PA could barely be heard above the din. We went through the usual round of songs and eventually came to a cover we did of "Afterglow." I was pretty annoyed with the noise by this stage, so I tweaked the volume on the Mellotron about five degrees and turned the choir on through the biggest and most saturated cathedral reverb you have ever heard, fading in on the pedal at the appropriate part of the song. I still recall the next moment as though it was happening right now; the noise in the bar ceased. Every clinking glass, every chinging till and every conversation simply stopped and all pairs or eyes in the room turned towards the stage in a shocked kind of disbelief. It was as though someone famous had just stepped into the room.

Duncan Goddard (Radio Massacre International, owner, M400 #1098)

I don't know exactly when I first heard it, but it must've been Moodies; probably *Nights in White Satin* or something off *Lost Chord*. King Crimson came much later, as did Yes and the rest of them. I wondered what the hell it was that wasn't remotely like the strings it pretended to be (my parents were both musicians so I knew what real violins, cellos, flutes and choirs ought to sound like) but somehow it still did the job better that anything else with a keyboard. Still does. By the time I knew what was going on inside the 'Tron, I'd been playing with 1/4" machines for ages (since age 8 or 9) and understood exactly how that sound became so intangible and special.

The eight-second thing never really bothers us, though there's a track on *Bothered Atoms*, a companion CD-R release to *Borrowed Atoms*, where Steve gets a bit carried away and the tapes run out on him. Eight seconds is quite a long time, musically, even to a band that's released 50-minute pieces. As for effects—what haven't we tried? I've never put much distortion on it, bar the overdrive on the Korg Leslie simulator. We've vocoded it, frozen it in delay lines and chopped it up, slowed it right down (the iceberg noises on "Frozen North" started out as 'Tron). Normally just a syncopated repeat and some huge reverb though. Little or no EQ, though some of the woodwinds can get a bit shrill sometimes. Oh, and it has a pull-switch on the pitch knob that takes it down an octave (this isn't a new idea, apparently, and ours got this mod so long ago I can't remember doing it). The pitch knob only goes a semitone now, because it's between the keyboard and the volume knob (which is daft) and we had one or two mishaps.

#1098 is the only 'Tron we own, but we've used and/or met another few 400's, discounting all the machines at Martin's (Smith) place or John's (Bradley) front room, the Cocteaus' machine, one at a studio in Crouch End, and Andy Thompson's (which shared our stage with #1098 in Holland a few weeks back). Adrian (Air Sculpture) has one, but it wouldn't work when we shared the bill at Jodrell Bank a few years ago.

In terms of sounds, there are seven frames right here next to me, some ex-TD (Tangerine Dream), some new, and some tapes that used to be on frames but aren't any more. I think I've heard most of the stock sounds.

No opinion on the Mark VI, since I haven't seen one or played one, and I don't want to get drawn into discussing it without the necessary first hand experience. I trust John and Martin, but opinion is so varied on what exactly the machine should behave like. Some people hate Ricky (Rickenbacker) guitars, I hate Gibsons personally, but it doesn't have anything to do with the build quality and it doesn't stop some fine players using them.

#1098 has never misbehaved on stage, though there a few tales in the liner notes of our new live release, *Upstairs Downstairs*, relating to moving it around—and a great picture of it on the cover.

Robert Cervero (M400 #1095)

On his first awareness of a Mellotron:

It was at a Moody Blues concert in late October, 1970, at Duke University, the Cameron Field House. I was bowled over. An otherworldly sound—thick, symphonic, moody, mind-stretching, heavenly, dominant. I had never heard anything like it, having been reared on the sounds of four-piece bands with two guitars, a bass, and a drummer.

On the "aha" experience:

Most definitely. It was sort of that thrilling disequilibria sensation one feels when taking a sharp dip on a roller coaster.

On limitations:

Not at all. The limitations are the very personality of the instrument. It's the eight-second sustain, wobbly, slightly out-of-tune sound of the Mellotron that makes it the unique, one-of-a-kind instrument that it is. I wouldn't want it any different. It's for this very reason that I've refrained from digital samples of Mellotrons—they're incapable of re-creating the slightly flawed signature sound of the Mellotron.

On recording techniques:

I like the sound of a Mellotron "unplugged," that is, stripped to the basics. I use slight reverb, however I'm pretty much a purist and prefer mainly the unvarnished sound of a 'Tron—warts and all.

On models owned:

M400, #1095. My website has a photo of my 'Tron: **http://www-dcrp.ced.berkeley.edu/cervero/music_miscellany.htm**

You can right-click and save the image. The sounds are 3-violins, sax, choir, brass, organ, gothic.

I've never performed on stage with one, thus I don't have any juicy stories. The most painful experience I had was in picking up my MKII at the San Francisco International Airport two years ago. After long awaiting its arrival from England, I went to the pick up station at United's air freight terminal. I saw it coming toward me on a forklift, dangling on the edges. I was grinning ear to ear in excitement when the forklift operator stopped abruptly in front of me and the Mellotron, protected only by its leather, wrap-around case, proceed to drop two feet. That was my first exposure to my new 'Tron—it was literally dropped in my lap. I had visions of it being destroyed. It turned out to be a pretty hearty machine. Only the tape rack really was knocked out of whack. Still, it wasn't how I wanted this relationship to begin. My advice is to spend extra money to get it properly packaged and delivered. My machine was in a large container mixed with other consigned packages. I wish it had been sent separately in its own wooden container.

Andy Thompson (owner, M400 #1145)

I think the first time I became aware of the Mellotron was when I went to see Led Zep's *The Song Remains the Same* at the cinema, in early 1977. I'd already heard the album, and I distinctly remember wondering where they put the string and flute sections! I was only 14, OK! At the relevant bits of the film ("The Rain Song" and "Stairway"), I realized that they were being played on a keyboard, and I really liked the sound. I remember noting the (credited) Mellotron on Rush's *2112*, and a couple of Black Sabbath albums (this was well before I discovered the Great God Prog), with maybe a few others (Hawkwind, Yes, Aerosmith), but I suspect my first real encounter with one was the first time I saw Limelight, a Rush-y three-piece from northern England, whose guitarist played one on a couple of tracks. I probably first saw Pallas around the same time (v. early '80s), and would've noted theirs, too. I don't think I can actually say I had that "aha!" moment, precisely, but seeing the Zeppelin film was probably the nearest thing to it!

On the limitations:

Ha-ha... how do they affect anybody?! If I'm writing stuff on it, I write to its limitations, but I've had problems in the band I'm in at the moment, where most of the parts I want to use it on weren't written for the instrument, and while using samples in rehearsal gets round the problem (well, several problems, actually!), it's going to be a pig to do the parts when we record. I suspect I'll have to use two tracks, switching from one to the other for long, sustained chords. It's called cheating. My machine is actually very reliable (it should be, it's been up to Martin & John's often enough), so the tape transport doesn't really cause any problems. Usually.

On recording techniques:

Just a bit of reverb—spring, preferably, but realistically, an old Alesis I've got knocking around. The only EQ I use is to stop the top end "shrieking." I've heard them put through Leslies, phasers, etc. but I prefer the "straight" sound of the machine, myself.

I own M400 number 1145, completed November '73. I saw an ad in Melody Maker (when they still had decent equipment ads) in September '85, I think, saying "Mellotron, £175", or similar. Of course nobody wanted them at the time, and I'd definitely caught the bug by then! I'd already played a friend's Mark II, and the ad caught my eye immediately. It was a bit of an impulse buy, 'cos I knew it was rather impractical, but, well, I just had to have it!

I seem to remember a bizarre train of events following, with the person at the other end of the phone telling me to go into Colchester (county of Essex, near London). I remember stopping in the town, but I'm not sure why. Maybe I had to get further instructions. It was all very odd, and I'll never know why it couldn't be more straightforward. Anyway, I was then directed to a permanent caravan park (a bit like an upmarket version of your trailer parks, I suppose), where I was given an address, a good few miles away. It was all most peculiar, but I don't remember ever thinking about giving up!

We (my brother and I) ended up at a small village near the extremely bland town of Braintree, in the north of the county. God knows how far we'd driven by this point, but I wasn't bloody giving up! The 'Tron was in an upstairs room in a dull, modern house, and as soon as I played it I realised that it was in rather less than perfect nick. The more notes I played, the more the pitch dropped—almost certainly a knackered motor board, I now know. Nonetheless, I wasn't going away empty-handed, and I rather naively assumed I'd be able to find someone to fix it. It also had exactly the three sounds I'd have chosen—strings, choir and flutes. £175 changed hands, and we somehow stuffed it into the back of my mother's small hatchback. It wasn't till we got back to London that I realised I didn't have the mains lead, and of course, I didn't have a phone number for the guys I'd bought it from! Luckily, I must've given them my address, 'cos it arrived in the post a couple of days later. Of course, Bulgin plugs were still available then, but it saved me a bit more expense.

To be honest, it's a slightly beaten-up looking white M400, like many others! Nothing special, as 'Trons go. As I said, the frame I got with it has flutes, 3 violins and 8-voice mixed choir, and I've just bought a Streetly frame, with cellos, string section and Mark II brass. I went through real agonies choosing the sounds, and I'm still not 100% convinced I got it right, but I'm stuck with 'em now.

I can't really comment on the new Mark VI without hearing one, to be honest. I applaud the idea of making new Mellotrons, but I feel the spec should be as close as possible to the original, really, with the only "upgrades" being those affecting its stability.

In all honesty, I've never actually played my own Mellotron live, although it's been gigged by a few other people since I've owned it. It's always behaved itself on stage, although the same can't always be said for its studio exploits. The best story I've heard regarding Mellotronic problems was from IQ's Martin Orford, who told me that he stopped gigging it when he found one of his roadies bumping it down a flight of stairs, one at a time. Ouch!

My chief problem with my machine seems to be persuading bands I'm in to let me use it—they all love the sound, but just see it as totally impractical, and invariably ask "Why can't you just use samples?" Philistines! Next impractical keyboard on my "wants" list: a Hammond C3. Now that's impractical!

Fritz Doddy (owner, M400 #1697)

I became aware of the Mellotron upon hearing Genesis' *Foxtrot* and shortly after that King Crimson's *In the Court of the Crimson King*. Initially I was drawn to these groups for their musicality and avant-garde approach to rock music. I was probably 14 years old at that time. Shortly after that Yes' *Fragile* came out, which also piqued my interest in this genre of music. Yes's *Close to the Edge* is the album that put me over the top. Today it still remains one of my favorite works. (Rick) Wakeman's dark and moody use of the Mellotron on that album started my love affair with this instrument. (Robert) Fripp was also a master of the dark, yet beautiful approach to the 'Tron.

I often find freedom in limitation. My career is as a composer and I compose mostly for TV ads and network identities, so I thrive on limitations. Not only are there the limitations you mentioned but the M400 has no sustain pedal, the classic "3 violins" are fairly out of tune from one end of the keyboard to the other and it is not velocity sensitive. The mechanical limitations are easy to deal with; the sonic limitations can be tricky. The 'Tron forces me to carefully examine my arrangement in any given piece of music, i.e., will the 'Tron's inherent tuning blend well with the other instruments? Will its timbre be contradictory or complimentary with the other instruments I have in mind? Can I build the arrangement so that the 'Tron can enter and exit naturally? These are great limitations and they enhance my arranging skills.

I always record my 'Tron with no effects, and through a tube pre-amp. My main recording environment is Digital Performer and I have found that the Waves Renaissance EQ is the only eq that works on the 'Tron. Since my only sounds are violins, flute and 8-voice choir, I have yet to find a need for reverb as these sounds, when played legato, don't need lengthening. If I need a thicker sound, I will double track the same sound slightly detuned and played slightly differently and then hard pan the two performances. I will often play a part with my right hand and change volume, tone and pitch in real time as I see fit.

I have only ever owned one 'Tron, and hopefully it won't be my last. I would love a Mark II. I have wanted a 'Tron since I was 16 or 17 years old. My wife promised me that one day she would buy me one and that was 20 years ago. My 'Tron acquisition started with my purchase of my Minimoog. After renovating that instrument, my youth caught up with me and I found myself wanting "that sound" for my professional life. Initially I answered some ads for people selling Mellotrons but never felt right about purchasing one unseen and in suspect condition. I then came across DK's site (Mellotron Archives) and the mellotronists list and I contacted Dave about purchasing a renovated 'Tron. Dave was unresponsive to my requests and that lead me to Streetly. Martin Smith was immediately helpful. After many emails with Martin (Smith) and Jerry Korb, I was convinced that buying a 'Tron from Streetly was the way to go. I cannot describe the childlike glee I felt when I loaded that beast in my van after I got it out of customs. I have had my 'Tron for almost two years now and not a day goes by when I don't stop and look at it and realize how fortunate I am to have one of these. I will soon be receiving my second rack of tapes and with it the same feeling all over again. My original rack has flute, 3 violins and 8-voice choir (no surprises there) and my new rack will have medieval woodwinds (very ugly/beautiful), M300B Strings and a custom split of one octave of bass accordion and cello the rest of the keyboard.

I have only ever played a 'Tron in the studio but the first time I heard one live was an epiphany of sorts. The local "great" cover band had one for their live shows and when I was old enough to see them perform, I specifically went to hear the 'Tron. What a treat to hear one live for the first time. The sound was so present. The keyboard player must have sensed my intrigue in the beast and let me play a few chords on it. Talk about power under the fingertips. From then on I was hooked. I make my living as a composer and I compose mostly for TV ads. When appropriate, I use my 'Tron in ads. I currently have a spot for BASF that features 3-violins as part of the arrangement.

Appendix A

The Sounds

Mellotron and Chamberlin Sound Libraries

Mellotron Mark I Leads

This is the selection of sounds from the Mark I masters Mellotron Archives received from Les Bradley in 1990. There may be older Mark I's with differences, especially in the left hand keyboard Rhythms and Fills section. There have been two other configurations listed for the left side in old literature, letters and the original Mellotron Booklet.

Mellotron Mark I Leads

	Track A	Track B	Track C
Station 1	Clarinet	Flute	Mandolin
Station 2	French Horn	Guitar	Organ
Station 3	Marimba	Piano	Vibraphone
Station 4	Trombone	Tenor Sax	Open Trumpet
Station 5	Hammond Organ	Trumpet/Trombone	Tibia Organ
Station 6	French Accordion	Reverb Organ	Church Organ

Mellotron Mark I Rhythms and Fills

	Track A	Track B	Track C
Station 1	Bossa Nova 'Cello and Violin Moving	Viennese Waltz Marimba Tremolo	Slow Waltz/Celeste
Station 2	Rumba/Guitar	Afro Cuban/Afro Cuban	Accordion Bass Notes Accordion
Station 3	Dixie Land/Trombone	Slow Foxtrot/Woodwinds	Foxtrot/Saxophone
Station 4	Church Organ/Church Organ	Cha-Cha/Swinging Flutes	Moving Bass/ 'Cello and Violin Chords
Station 5	Foxtrot 2/Moving Piano Chords	Bolero/3 Clarinets	Tango/Sound FX
Station 6	Jazz Foxtrot/Piano Chords	Samba/Electronic Organ	Fast Jazz Bass Sound FX

Mellotron Mark II Leads

This is the selection of sounds from the Mark II masters Mellotron Archives received from Les Bradley in 1990. There may be older Mark II's with differences, especially in the left hand keyboard Rhythms and Fills section. There have been two other configurations listed for the left side in old literature, letters and the original Mellotron Booklet.

Mellotron Mark II Leads

	Track A	Track B	Track C
Station 1	Flute	Rock Guitar	Organ
Station 2	3 Violins	Brass	Tenor Sax
Station 3	Acoustic Guitar	Piano	Vibraphone
Station 4	Trumpet	Muted Brass	Mandolin
Station 5	Hammond Organ	Harpsichord	Tibia Organ
Station 6	Accordion	French Accordion	Church Organ

Mellotron Mark II Rhythms and Fills

	Track A	Track B	Track C
Station 1	Bossa Nova 'Cello and Violin Moving	Viennese Waltz Marimba Tremolo	Slow Waltz/Celeste
Station 2	Rumba/Guitar	Cuban/Afro Cuban	Accordion Bass Notes Accordion
Station 3	Dixie Land/Trombone	Slow Foxtrot/Woodwinds	Quickstep/Saxophone
Station 4	Church Organ Church Organ	Cha-Cha/Swinging Flutes	Moving Bass 'Cello and Violin Chords
Station 5	Reverberated Organ Reverberated Organ	Bolero/3 Clarinets	Tango/Piano Chords
Station 6	Slow Jazz Bass Blues Beat Rhythm in F	Samba/6/8 Tempo in F	Fast Jazz Bass/Twist in C

Mellotron Mark II KFF Leads

The Mark II Rhythms and Fills, with all of their charm, are not for everyone. After many requests to offer an alternate selection, Mellotron Archives compiled a new set of Mark II leads. This set, while not "period" for a Mark II, makes many of the M400 and M300 sounds available.

Mellotron Mark II KFF Leads

	Track A	Track B	Track C
Station 1	Pipe Organ	8 Voice Choir	2 Brass
Station 2	Boy's Choir	Male Choir	Female Choir
Station 3	Oboe	Bassoon	Alto Sax
Station 4	Solo Violin	Solo Viola	'Cello
Station 5	Strings 1	Mark II Brass	16 Violins
Station 6	Pizzicato Violins	M300 Strings	Clavichord

Mellotron Mark II Alternate Leads

As well as being able to supply replacement tapes for Mark II's, Streetly Electronics offers alternative lead tapes made up from any 18 sounds from the M300/400 library in any order. These sets are usually used to replace the Rhythms and Fills tapes on the left hand keyboard (which can sound a bit dated), although the right hand ones can be replaced as well. These choices also apply to replacement tapes for the M300.

Mk II Violins, M400 Violins (EQ'd Mk II), M300 A & B Strings, Violin, Viola, 'Cello, String Section, String Section–no 'Cello, Classic Strings, Dickstrings M300A & Viola-especially for Mike Dickson Mark II, Combined Brass, Muted Brass, Trumpet, Trombone, Mixed Brass B, GC3 Brass, Moog Brass, Solo Oboe, 2 Trombone/2 Trumpet, Bassoon, Mk II Flute, Cor Anglais/Oboe split (new Oboe), Soprano Sax, Tenor Sax Alto Sax, 2 Tenor/2 Alto Saxes, Mk I Clarinet, Bass Clarinet, Piccolo, Recorder, Male Choir, Female Choir Ian McDonald Classical Flute, French Horn, Boy's Choi,r 8 Voice Choir, Combined Choir, Piano, Gothic Orchestra, Medieval Woodwind, Vibes (w/ vibrato), Electric Guitar, Spanish Guitar, St. John's Wood Church Organ, Italian Accordion, Mandolin, Marimba, Glock/Tubular Bells, split Woodwind 2 (incl. French Horn & piccolo for a very smooth sound)

New for 2000:

Steve Hackett's Sustained Electric Guitar, Tony Levin's NS Electric Cello, Adrian Belew's Sustained Electric Guitar, Ric Sander's Electric Violin, Gordon Gilstrap's Guitar Harmonics, Ray Jung's Fretless Bass, Fairlight Aah1, Fairlight Swannee, Fairlight Saxy, Plucked Piano, Ebow, Twelve-string, Any Mk II or M300 sound, Any special tapes you require (if viable)

Mellotron 300 Leads

The tapes for the 300 come in two versions, tape set A and tape set B, from Mellotron Archives. Each machine can only have one set at a time, although they are interchangeable. The Rhythm selections were not available at the time of printing. The first listing is the 'A' set; the second, the 'B' Set.

Mellotron 300 Leads		
Tape set A		
	Track A	Track B
Station 1	Flute (no vibrato)	Trombone
Station 2	Piano	Vibes (slow)
Station 3	Clarinet	Organ
Station 4	Spanish Guitar	Organ (w/ vibrato)
Station 5	Organ	Vibes
Station 6	Violin	Harpsichord
Tape Set B		
	Track A	Track B
Station 1	Saxophone	Flute
Station 2	Vibes	Clarinet
Station 3	Trombone	Violin
Station 4	Harpsichord	Spanish Guitar
Station 5	Hammond (w/ Leslie)	Hammond
Station 6	Piano	Organ

Mellotron 400 Sounds

As offered by Mellotron Archives

3 Violins, 16 Violins, Violin, Viola, 'Cello, Alto Sax, Trumpet, Trombone, French Horn, Oboe, English Horn Bassoon, Recorder, Clarinet, Flute, Vibes (w/ vibrato), Guitar (nylon), Guitar (steel), Mandolin, Male Choir Female Choir, 8 Voice Mixed Choir, Boy's Choir, M300A Strings (a la Barclay James Harvest), M300B Strings (2 violins, 2 violas), String Section ('cello, viola, 3 violins mixed), String Section II (viola, 3 violins, solo violin), Mark II Brass, 2 Brass (split keyboard 2 Trombone/2 Trumpet), GC3 Brass, 2 Saxes, split keyboard–2 Tenor/2 Alto, Tenor Sax, Woodwinds (oboe, flute, clarinet, bassoon), Pipe Organ, Piano Woodwinds II (no bassoon), Clavichord, Celeste, Accordion, Hammond C-3 (w/ percussion and slow Leslie), Wine Glasses, Jack Bruce, Female Solo Voice, Sound FX, Black Sabbath Sound FX, Tangerine Dream Sound FX, Roxy Music Sound FX

Sound Effects

These are the sounds effects as offered on the Mellotron Mark II SFX units supplied to the BBC. Mellotron Archives has these sounds available for any model.

Turbo Prop, 4 Engine Piston, Saloon Car, Sports Car, Large Jet, Helicopter, 4 Stroke Motorcycle, Land Rover, Small Jet, Single Engine Piston, Lorry, 2 Stroke Vespa, Electronics, Electric Train, Tractor, Applause & Chat, Radiophonics, Steam Train, Industrial Effects, Musical Effects, Diesel Train, Aircraft, Airfield Comet IV, Viscount, Tiger Moth, Animals, Church Bells, Bells (misc.), Birds, Chime Buzzer, Clocks, Crashes & Bangs, Quiet Atmosphere, Chatter, Footsteps, Laughter & Applause, Hard Surface, Pavement, Atmosphere London, Horses, Household, Toilet, Insects, Ships, Boats, Barge, etc., Telephones, Motor Vehicles (interior), Steam Trains (exterior), Diesel (Interior), Underground, Suburban Electric, Gunfire, War Battle, Fireworks, Doors, Rowing, Guns, Metal Crashes, Misc., Door Creak, Shots & Crashes, Sea, Water Splashes/Swimming, Hooters, Launch, Sail Ship, Cup & Drawer, Glass & Explosion, Water, Chopping Wood, etc., Train Crash, Crowds, Football, Boxing, Swords, Ice & Greyhound, Fight, Cricket, Cuckoo Clock, T.T. Racing, Car Racing (Le Mans), Baby, Comical Feet, Tennis, Var. Sports, Lifts, Hovercraft, Glass, Crashes, etc., Children, Foreign Crowds, Angry, Excited Crowds, Marching, Sirens, Docks, Diving, Horns, Air Raid, Goon Comic Noises, Wind, Rain, Thunder, Betting Shop

Chamberlin Sound Selections

The Chamberlin M series (from Mellotron Archives) has six selections of two sounds each. The guard band in between the two tracks (A and B) of the stereo heads skips one track of the 1/2" 8-track tape giving the following order:

8Trk# 1 = Chamberlin Trk 6a
8Trk# 2 = Chamberlin Trk 5a
8Trk# 3 = Chamberlin Trk 6b and 4a & 3a
8Trk# 4 = Chamberlin Trk 5b
8Trk# 5 = Chamberlin Trk 4b and 2a & 1a
8Trk# 6 = Chamberlin Trk 3b
8Trk# 7 = Chamberlin Trk 2b
8Trk# 8 = Chamberlin Trk 1b

As you can see, tracks 3, 4, 5 and 6 are available for two pairs each. For example, Selection 1 would give you tracks 1 and 3, selection 2 would give you tracks 2 and 4 and selection 3 gives you tracks 3 (again) and 5.

The 3 Violins sound is the only sound that is shared by the Mellotron and always has been. This is the one sound from the original Chamberlin library that the Bradley Brothers and Eric Robinson kept for Mellotron tape production.

Chamberlin M Series Patches

Male Voice (solo)	Female Voice (solo)
Alto sax	Tenor Sax
Trumpet	Trombone
French Horn	Do Wah
Slur Trombone	Muted Trumpet
Marimba	Piano
Vibes (w/ vibrato)	Flute
Bass Clarinet	Oboe
Bassoon	Temple Blocks
Slur Guitar	Banjo
Steel Guitar	Bells (Glockenspiel)
3 Violins	Cello
Dixieland Band Phrase	Trombone Sound Effects
Organ	Kinura Organ
Tibia Organ	Harpsichord
Electric Harpsichord	Flute/String/Organ
Pizzicato Violins	Harp Solo
Guitar	Mandolin

Appendix B

Advertisements

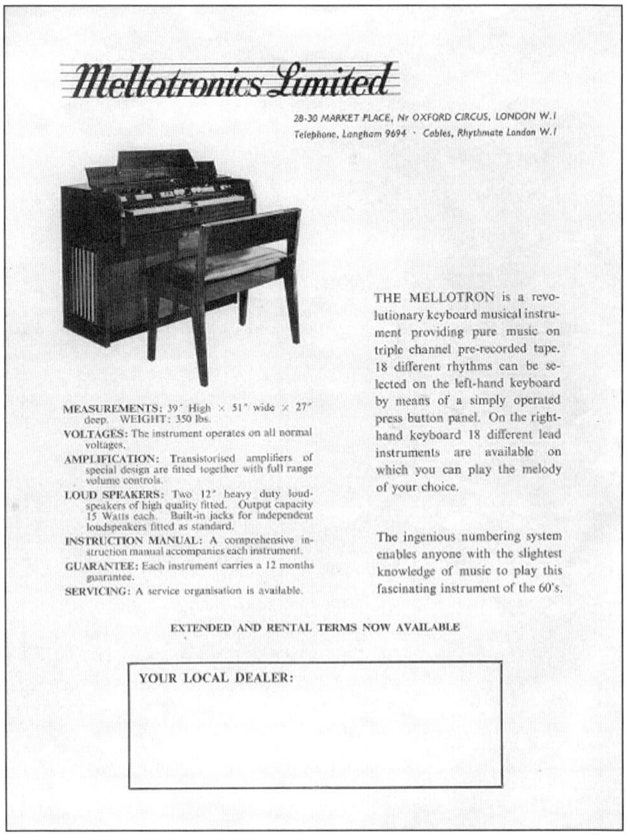

Mellotronics ads for the Mellotron Mark II

Mellotronics ad for the Mellotron M300

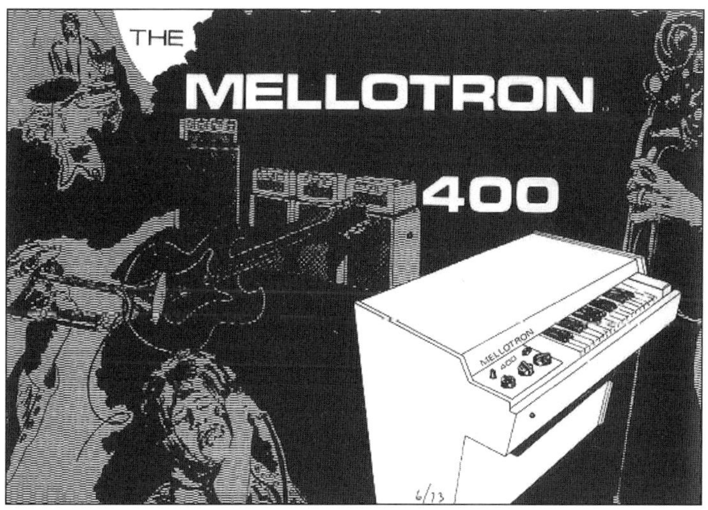

Cover of Mellotron M400 catalog

Cover of Mellotron M400 Owner's Manual

Dallas Arbiter/Dallas Music/Sound Sales ad for Mellotron M400

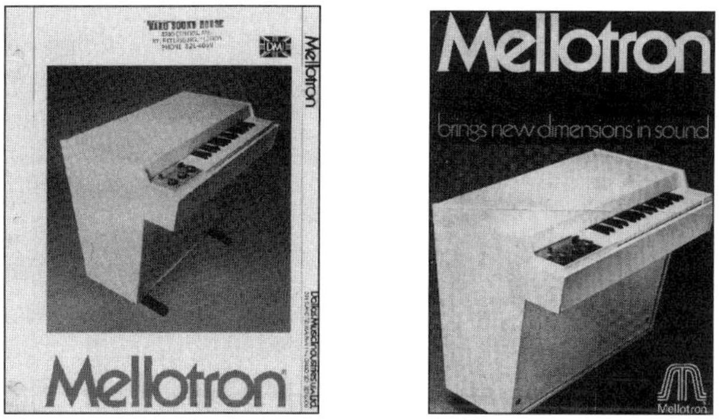

Dallas Arbiter/Dallas Music/Sound Sales ads for Mellotron M400

Mellotronics ad for the Mellotron Mark V

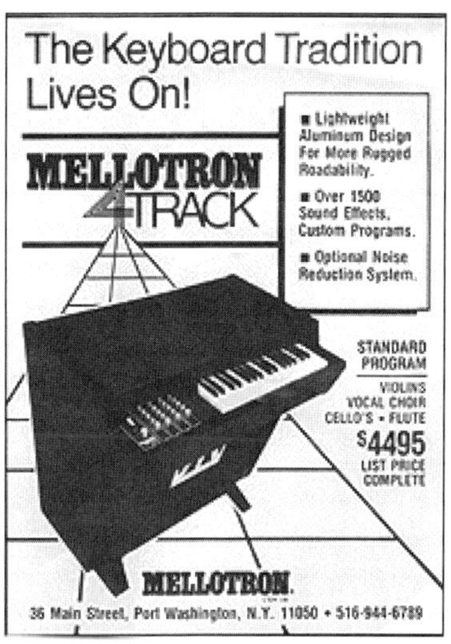

Mellotron USA ad for the Mellotron 4-Track

Streetly ad for Novatron 400FX Sounds Effects Console

Streetly ad for the Novatron T550

Appendix C

The Albums

For other detailed information, please also see Andy Thompson's web page at:
http://freespace.virgin.net/andy.thompson

PART I: From Mellotron Archives Newsletter #6

Abba–1st US LP
Abba–Ring Ring (Sweden)
Abba–Waterloo
Aerosmith–Pump 1991
Aerosmith–Angel
Afghan Whigs–Gentlemen 1993
Agamon–Open Up Your Eyes (Sweden) 1993
Akasha–Akasha (Norway)
Alf Emil Elk Joy And Breath Of Eternity (Norway)
Alice Cooper–Billion Dollar Babies (US)
Amazing Blondel–England (UK) 1972
American Music Club Mercury
Amon Duul II–Wolf City (Germany)
Anekdoten–Vermod (Sweden) 1993
Anka, Paul–You're Having My Baby
Ange Au Dela Du Delire (France) 1974
Ange–Caricatures (France) 1972
Ange–Emile Jacotey (France) 1975
Ange–Guet Apens (France) 1978
Ange–Le Cimetiere Des Arlequins (France) 1973
Ange–Par Les Fils De Mandrin (France) 1976
Angel–1st and 2nd LP's (US)
Angel–Angel (US) 1975
Angel–Helluva Band (US) 1976
Anglagard–Hybris (SWEDEN) 1993
Aphrodites Child–666
Apocalypsis–Apocalypsis
April Wine–Like A Lover, Like A Song (Canada)
Argent–Circus (UK) 1975

Argent–Encore
Argent–Nexus
Arthur Browns Kingdom Come–The Whirlpool (UK)
Arthur Browns Kingdom Come–Journey (UK)
Arthur Browns Kingdom Come–Galactic 200 Dossier
Arthur Browns Kingdom Come–Arthur Browns
Kingdom Come
Arti + Mestieri–Live (Italy)
Ascencion
Ashra Correlations (Germany) 1979
Asia–Asia 1979
Asia–Armed To The Teeth 1980
Asia Minor–Between Flesh And Divine 1980
Atlantis Philharmonic–Atlantis Philharmonic (US)
Attaway, Murray–In Trhall
Atila–Intencion (Spain)
Atlas–Bla Vardag (Sweden)
Atlantis Philharmonic–Atlantis Philharmonic (US) 1974
Aubrery Small–Aubrery Small (UK)
Axis–Axis (Greece)
Azahar–Elixir (Spain) 1977
B-52s–Cosmic Thing
Babe Ruth–various lp's
Badger–One Live Badger
Balletiro Sadimacchia–Balletir Sadimacchia (Italy)
Bang!–Music
Bangels
Barclay James Harvest–Baby James Harvest (UK) 1972
Barclay James Harvest–Barclay James Harvest 1970
Barclay James Harvest–Every One Is Everybody Else 1974
Barclay James Harvest–Gone To Earth 1977
Barclay James Harvest–Live (UK)
Barclay James Harvest–Live Tapes 1 978
Barclay James Harvest–Octoberon 1976
Barclay James Harvest–Once Again 1971
Barclay James Harvest–Other Short Stories 1971
Barclay James Harvest–Time Honoured Ghosts 1975
Barefoot Jerry–You Can't Get Off With Your Shoes On (US)
Barone, Richard–Primal Dream 1992
Barone, Richard–Clouds Over Eden 1993
Bauman, Peter -Romance 76 (Germany) 1976
Beach Boys–Wild Honey 1968
Beatles–Magical Mystery Tour
Beatles–White Album
Beck, Bogert, Appice–Beck, Bogert, Appice
Beck, Bogert, Appice–Oh To Love You (US/UK)
Bee Gees–First (Australia)
Beggars Opera–Get Your Dog Off Me
Beggars Opera–Pathfinder(UK) 1972
Beggars Opera–Silver Peacock
Beggars Opera–Time Machine
Beggars Opera–Waters Of Change 1971
Berry, Heidi–Heidi Berry
Bi Kyo Ran–Parallax (Japan) 1983
Big Star–No 1 Record (US)
Blackfish–Blackfish
Black Sabbath–Volume 4 (UK)
Black Sabbath–Sabbath Bloody Sabbath
Black Sabbath–Sabotage
Black Sabbath–Technical Ecstasy
Blackmore's Rainbow–Catch The Rainbow (UK)
Blair, Jim–Turn The Tide 1986
Blocco–Mentale Poa (Itlay) 1973
Blocco–Mentale Iloa (Italy(
Bloque–Bloque 1978
Bloque–Musica Para Le Libertao (Spain) 1981
Blues Project (Al Cooper)–Live Reunion Album
Bond, Graham–Sound of '65
Bond, Graham–There's A Bond Between Us
Bonilla, Marc–E E Ticket
Bowie, David–Space Oddity (UK)
Bowie, David–Diamond Dogs (UK)
Box Tops–The Letter
Bregent Partir–Pour Ailleurs (Canada)
Brosel Maschine–Brosel Maschine
Brown, Duncan–Duncan Brown
Brown, Duncan–Wild Places
Buccheri, Francesco–Journey (Italy)
Buccheri, Francesco–2nd Journey (Italy)
Budgie–If I Were Brittania I'd Waive The Rules
Budgie–Squawk (UK)
Buck Pets-, The Mercurotones

Busser–Movies (Switzerland)
Cai Mas Alla De Nuestras Mentes (Spain)
Calliope–Citta Di Froniera (Italy) 1993
Calliope–La Eerra Del Grande Occhi (Italy) 1992
Camel–Camel (UK) 1973
Camel–Mirage
Campo Di Marte–Campo Di Marte (Italy)
Capability Brown–Voice (UK) 1973
Capaldi, Jim–Seagull (UK)
Captain Beefheart–Doc At The Radar Station
Caravan–In The Land Of Grey and Pink (UK) 1971
Cargoe–Cargoe (US)
Carmen–Fandangos In Space (US) 1973
Cathedral–Stained Glass Stories
Cave Dogs–Soul Martini
Celeste–Celeste (Italy)
Celluloid–Neptune (UK)
Ceremony
Cherry Five–Cherry Five (Italy)
Cherry Five–Country Grave Yard
Chilliwack–Ridin' High
Chicago–VII
Cire D'Ammicco–Ciro D'Ammicco (Italy)
Cirkus–One (UK)
Citta Frontale–El Tor (Italy)
Clearlight Symphony–Clearlight Symphony (France)
Clearlight Symphony–Forever Blowing Bubbles (France)
Climax Blues Band–Mum's The Word (UK)
CMU–Space Cabaret (UK)
Coda–Sounds Of Passion (Holland)
Colonel Elliott and The Lunatics–Interstellar Reggae Drive 1974
Connoly, Robert–Plateau (Canada)
Cosmos Factory–An Old Castle Of Transylvania (Japan)
Costello, Elvis–Mighty Like A Rose 1992
Costello, Elvis–Spike
Coto En Pel–Holocaust (Spain) 1975
Court Of Appeal
Convenant Natures Devine Reflection 1993
Crack In The Sky–Live Sky
Crack In The Sky–Safety In Numbers
Cream–Goodbye
Cressida–Asylum (UK) 1971
Cressida–Cressida (UK) 1970
Cult, The–Sonic Temple
Cure, The–Wish
Curved Air–Conditioning (UK)
Curved Air–Cut (UK) 1973
Curved Air–Phastamagoria (UK) 1971
Curved Air–Midnight Wire
Curved Air–Airborne
Dallaglio Sera Mattina (Italy)
Dalton Rifussioni–Idea D'Infinito (Italy) 1971
Danzig–Danzig 2/ Lucifuge
Delirium III (Italy)
Delirium III (Italy) 1973
Dice–Four Riders Of The Apocalypse
Dice–Dice (Sweden)
Dinosaur Jr-. Green Mind
Don Bradshaw–Leather Distance Between Us (UK)
Dragon–Dragon (Belgium)
Dragonwyck
Druid–Fluid Druid (UK) 1976
Druid–Toward The Sun (UK) 1975
Dukes Of Stratosphear
Dyzan–Electric Silence (Germany)
E–Broken Toy Shop
Earth And Fire–Atlantis (Holland)
Earth And Fire–From The End Til The Beginning (Holland)
Earth And Fire–Memories (Holland)
Earth And Fire–Song Of The Marching Children (Holland)
Earth And Fire–To The World Of The Future (Holland)
Earthstar–French Skyline 1979
Earthstar–Humans Only 1982
Easter Island–Now And Then (US)
Eberhard Schoener–Video Magic (German)
Eberhard Schoener–Flashback
Eberhard Schoener–Bali Agung
Eberhard Schoener–Time Square (German)
Edgar Winter Group–Shock Treatment (US)
Eduardo Bort–Eduardo Bort (Spain) 1975

Electric Sandwich–Electric Sandwich (Germany)
Eloy–Ocean (Germany) 1977
Eloy–Power And Passion (Germany) 1975
Emergency–Early In The Morning
Emtidi Saat
Enuff Is Enuff
England–Garden Shed (UK) 1977
Epidaurus–Earthly Paradise (German)
Epitaph–Visions (Germany)
Ertlif–Ertlif (Switzerland) 1972
Ethos Ardour (US) 1976
Ekseption–Ekseption 1969
Ekseption–Beggar Julia's Time Trip
Ekseption–3
Ekseption–00.04
Ekseption–5
Ekseption–Trinity
Eyes Of Blue–Crossroads Of Time (UK)
Eyes Of Blue–Fields Of Ardath (UK)
FM–City Of Fear
Fairfield Parlor–From Home To Home (UK)
Faithful Breath–Fading Beauty (Germany) 1973
Fantasy–Paint A Picture (UK) 1973
Fantasy–Beyond The Beyond (UK) 1974
Far East–Family The Cave Down Through The Earth (Japan) 1975
Fennelly, Michael–Lane Changer (US)
Fields–Fields (UK)
Finch–Glory Of Inner Force, Beyond Expression
Finch–Gallions Of Passion
Flamin' Groovies–Take Me Back
Flash–Out Of Our Hands
Fleetwood Mac–Bare Trees
Flint–You'll Never Be The Same (US)
Focus–Moving Waves (Holland)
Focus–Hamburger Concerto
Focus–Ship Of Memories
Foggy–Simple Gifts (UK) 1972
Formas–Largos Suenos (Spain) 1981
Formula 3–La Grande Casa (Italy) 1973
Froese, Edgar–Ages (Germany) 1978
Froese, Edgar–Ypsilon In Malaysian Pale (Germany) 1975
Froese, Edgar–Aqua (Germany) 1974
Froese, Edgar–Macula Transfer (Germany) 1976
Fuhrs And Frohling–Ammerland (Germany) 1978
Fusioon–Minorisa (Spain)
Future Shock–Future Shock (UK)
Galahad
Garybaldi–Nuda (Italy)
G. Men–G. Men (Italy) 1974
Genesis–A Trick Of The Tail (UK) 1976
Genesis–Foxtrot (UK) 1972
Genesis–Genesis Live (UK) 1973
Genesis–Nursery Crime (UK) 1971
Genesis–Selling England By The Pound (UK) 1973
Genesis–The Lamb Lies Down On Broadway (UK) 1974
Genesis–Trespass (UK) 1970
Genesis–Wind And Wuthering (UK) 1976
Gentle Giant–Acquiring The Taste (UK) 1971
Gentle Giant–Gentle Giant (UK) 1970
Gentle Giant–In A Glass House (UK) 1973
Gentle Giant–Three Friends (UK) 1972
Gentle Giant–Octopus
George Gruntz–2001 Keys-Piano Conclave (Switzerland)
Gerano–Empty Lie, Empty Dream (Japan)
Gerano–Gerano (Japan)
Giganti–Terra In Bocca (Italy)
Gladstone–Song Bird (US)
Goblin–Il Fantastico Viaggio Del Begarozzo
Goblin–Suspiria (Italy)
Godfrey, Robert John–Fall Of Hyperion (UK) 1974
Golden Earring–Seven Tears (Holland)
Golden Earring–Wall Of Dolls (Holland)
Gong–You
Goro Ohmi & Big Mouth–Guin Saga (Japan)
Goro Ohmi & Big Mouth–Guin Saga II (Japan)
Goro Ohmi & Big Mouth–Graffiti (Japan)
Gracious–Gracious (UK) 1970
Gracious–This Is (UK) 1971
Granada–Espan Ano 75 (Spain) 1975
Granada–Habla De Una Tierra (Spain) 1975
Grancher, Philippe–3000 Miles Away (France)
Granicus–Twilight (UK)

Grapes Of Wrath–These Days
Gravy Train–Ballad Of A Peaceful Man (UK) 1971
Gravy Train–Staircase To The Day(UK) 1974
Greenslade, Dave–Cactus Choir (UK) 1976
Greenslade–Bedside Manners Are Extra (UK) 1973
Greenslade–Greenslade (UK) 1973
Greenslade–Spyglass Guest (UK) 1974
Greenslade–Time And Tide (UK) 1975
Greenslade–Cosmogony Of The Pantateuch
Griffin–Raindances
Griffin–Treason
Grobschnitt–Ballerman(Germany) 1974
Grobschnitt–Jumbo (Germany) 1975
Grobschnitt–Merry Go Round (Germany) 1979
Grobschnitt–Rockpommels Land (Germany) 1977
Grobschnitt–Solar Music Live (Germany) 1978
Grobschnitt–The Excursion Of Father Smith (Germany)
Grobschnitt–Volle Molle (Germany) 1980
Groundhogs–Hogwash (UK)
Groundhogs–Snowstorm (UK)
Groundhogs–Solid (UK)
Groundhogs–Who Will Save The World (UK) 1972
Group Therapy–Wait
Gualberta Vericuistos (Spain) 1976
Hackett, Steve–Voyage Of The Acolyte (UK) 1975
Hackett, Steve–Please Don't Touch (UK) 1976
Hackett, Steve–Spectral Mornings (UK) 1979
Hackett, Steve–Defector (UK) 1980
Hackett, Steve–Cured
Hall & Oats–Abandoned Luncheonette (US)
Hammer, Jan–Melodies (US)
Hammer, Jan–The First Seven Days (US)
Hammil, Peter–In Camera
Hammil, Peter–Chameleon In The Shadow Of Night
Hammil, Peter–The Silent Corner and The Empty Stage
Hancock, Herbie–Sextant (US)
Hardie, Sebastian–
Hardie, Sebastian–Windchase (Australia)
Hardie, Sebastian–Four Moments
Harmonium–L Heptade 1976
Harmonium–Les Cinq Saisons
Harrison, George–Wonderwall (UK)
Hawkwind–Hall Of The Mountain Grill (UK) 1974
Hawkwind–Warrior On The Edge Of Time (UK) 1975
Head East–Flat As A Pancake
Heartsfield -Shine On
Heldon Allez Teia (France)
Helmerson, Anders–End Of Illusion (Sweden)
Heptade (Canada)
Hiraklis Se Allous–Kosmous (Greece)
Holding Pattern–Majestic (US)
Home–Pause For A Hoarse Horse (UK)
Hot Legs (10CC)–Hall Think School Stinks (UK)
Hunka Munka–Dedicato A Giovanni G (Italy) 1972
Hunter, Ian–Ian Hunter
Hunter, Ian–All American Alien Boy
Hush–Hush (US)
Hydravion–Hydravion (France) 1978
I Pooh–Parsifal (Italy) 1973
Ibio–Cueves De Altamira (Spain)
Ibis–Sun Supreme
Idle Race–Best Of (UK)
Ides Of March–World Woven
I Dik Dik–Suite Per Una Donna Assolutamente Relative (It)
Il Balletto Di Bronzo–YS (Italy)
Illusion–Illusion (Italy) 1978
Illusion–Out Of The Mist (Italy) 1977
Iman Califato–Independiere (Spain)
Indescribably Delicious–Indescribably Delicious
Indian Summer–Indian Summer (UK)
IQ–Tales From The Lush Attic (UK) 1983
IQ–The Wake(UK) 1987
I Signori Della Galassia–Qualcofa Si Crea Nulla Fi
Distrugge (Italy)
Jackson, Michael–Dangerous 1992
Jane–Here We Are (Germany) 1973
Jarre, Michael–Oxygene (France)
Jelly Fish–Spilt Milk
Jet–Jet (UK) 1975
Jethro Tull–Aqualung (UK)
Jethro Tull–Living In The Past
JoJo Gunne–Jumpin The Gunne (US)

Jonesy–Growing(UK) 1973
Jonesy–Keeping Up (UK) 1973
Jonesy–No Alternative (UK) 1972
John, Elton–Goodbye Yellow Brick Road (UK)
John, Elton–Caribou
John, Elton–A Single Man
John, Elton–Greatest Hits
John, Elton–Don't Shoot Me...
John, Elton–Captain Fantasic
John, Elton–Rock Of The Westies
John, Elton–Blue Eyes
Jose Cid–10000 Anos Depois Entre Venus E Marto
Jumbo (Italy)
Jumbo–Vietato Al Minori Di 18 Anni? (Italy) 1974
Kaipa (Sweden)
Kantner, Slick, Frieberg–Baron Von Tolbooth And The Chrome Nun
Kayak–Kyak (Holland)
Kayak–Royal Bed Bouncer (Holland)
Kayak–See See The Sun (Holland) 1973
Kayak–The Last Encore
Kayak–The Starlight Dancer
Kayak–Periscope Life
Kedama–Kedama (Switzerland)
Kennedy–Flying Ship
Kennedy–Twinilling NASA (Japan)
Kestral–Kestral (UK)
King Crimson–In The Court Of The Crimson King (UK)
King Crimson–In The Wake Of Poseidon (UK)
King Crimson–Islands (UK)
King Crimson–Larks Tongues In Aspic (UK)
King Crimson–Lizard (UK)
King Crimson–Red (UK)
King Crimson -Starless And Bible Black (UK)
King Crimson -USA (UK)
Kingdom Come–Journey (UK) 1973
Kingdom Come–Kingdom Come (UK) 1972
Kingdom Come–Superficial Roadblocks (UK)
King Pin Meh (Germany)
Kinks–Lola
Kinks–Arthur
Kinks–Village Green
Kinks–Kink Kronikles
Kite, The–The Kite
Kitaro–various lp's
Klaatu–Klaatu (Canada)
Klaus Schulze–X (Germany)
Kraftwerk–Radio Activity (Germany) 1975
Kraftwerk–Trans Europe Express (Germany) 1977
Kravitz, Lenny–Mama Said
Kravitz Lenny–Are You Gonna Go My Way
Kyrie Eleison–The Fountain Beyond The Sunrise (Austria)
Landberk–Lonely Land (Sweden) 1991
Latte E Miele–Passio Secundum Matheum (Italy)
Latte E Miele–Papillon
La Botegga Dell Arte–La Botegga Dell Arte
La Botegga Dell Arte–Dentro
Lennon, John–Walls And Bridges
Lennon, John–Mind Games
Lennon Julian–Help Yourself
Le Orme–Contrappunti (Italy) 1974
Le Orme–Felona And Sorona (Italy) 1973
Le Orme–Smogmagica (Italy) 1975
Le Orme–Verita Nascoste (Italy) 1976
Le Orme–Uomo Di Pezza
Leb I Sol Rucni Rad (Yugoslavia)
Led Zeppelin–Houses Of The Holy (UK)
Led Zeppelin–Physical Graffiti (UK)
Led Zeppelin–Song Remains The Same (UK)
Leviathan–Leviathan (US) 1974
Lift–Caverns Of Your Brain (US)
Light–The Story Of Moses (Holland)
Limelight–Limelight (UK)
Limelight–Future Earth (UK) 1980
Liquid Jesus–Pour In The Sky
Little Free Rock–Little Free Rock (UK)
Los Canarios–Ciclos (Spain) 1974
Los Lobos–Kiko
Lucifers Friend–Where The Groupies Killed The Blues
Lynyrd Skynyrd–Pronounced
Machiavel Mechanical–Moonbeams (Belgium) 1978
Mahogony Rush–IV (Canada)

Malo–Malo (US)
Mandala Band–The Eye Of The Vendor (UK) 1978
Manfred Mann's Earth Band–Nightingales And Bombers (UK) 1975
Manfred Mann's Earth Band–Solar Fire (UK) 1973
Manfred Mann's Earth Band–The Good Earth (UK) 1974
Manfred Mann's Earth Band–Roaring Silence
Mann, Aimee–Whatever
Manzanera, Phil–Diamond Head (UK)
Marble Orchard–Agent Invisible
Marianus–Visions From Out Of The Blue
Marsupilami–Arena (UK)
Martz, Jason–The Pillory (US) 1981
Matching Mole–Matching Mole
Matching Mole–The Little Red Album
Matter–Matter (US)
Mauve Sideshow–Mauve Sideshow
Mauve Sideshow–Meet Me In The Wasteland
McCartney, Paul–Red Rose Speedway
McCartney, Paul–Wings Over America
McCartney, Paul–McCartney II
McCartney, Paul–McCartney
McCartney, Paul–Pipes Of Peace
McCartney, Paul–Off The Ground
Meadow–The Friendship
Merryweather, Neil–Spacerangers
Method–Method 1976
Miguel Rios–La Huerta Atomica (Spain)
Minotaurus–Fly Away (Germany)
Montrose–We're Going Home
Moody Blues–A Question Of Balance (UK) 1970
Moody Blues–Caught Live + 5 (UK)
Moody Blues–Days Of Future Passed (UK) 1967
Moody Blues–Every Good Boy Deserves Favour (UK) 1971
Moody Blues–In Search Of The Lost Chord (UK) 1968
Moody Blues–Long Distance Voyager (UK)
Moody Blues–Octave (UK)
Moody Blues–On The Threshold Of A Dream (UK) 1969
Moody Blues–Seventh Sojourn (UK) 1972
Moody Blues–To Our Childrens Childrens Children (UK) 1969
Moody Blues–The Keys Of The Kingdom
Moraz, Patrick–The Story Of i (Switzerland)
Morio Inada & Be Mi Family (Japan)
Morse Code–Je Suis Les Temps (Canada)
Morse Code–Le Marche Des Hommes (Canada)
Morse Code–Procreation (Canada)
Mountain–Avalanche (US)
Mountain–Climbing (US)
Mountain–Nantucket Sleigh Ride (US)
Mugen Leda–En Le Cygne (Japan)
Multi Story East West (UK)
Museo Rosenbach–Della Natura (Italy)
Museo Rosenbach–Zarathustra
Mythos–Dreamlab(Germany) 1975
Mythos–Strange Guys (Germany) 1976
Neal, Chris–Winds Of Isis (Australia)
Nektar–Journey To The Center Of The Eye (UK) 1971
Nektar–Sounds Like This 1970
Nessie–Head In The Sand (Belgium)
Nessie–The Tree (Belgium)
Netherworld–In The Following Half Light
New England–New England
New Order
New Riders Of Purple Sage–Brujo
Newman, Tom–Fairie Symphony (UK) 1977
Niemen–Aerolit (Poland)
Niemen–Aeroliz (Poland)
Niemen–Katharsis (Poland)
Nightwinds–Nightwinds (Canada)
Nilsson, Harry–Nilsson Schmilsson
Northern Pikes–Neptune
Novalis–Banished Bridge (Germany) 1973
Novalis–Branoeng (Germany) 1977
Novalis–Konzerte (Germany) 1977
Novalis–Novalis (Germany) 1975
Novalis–Sommerabend (Novalis) 1976
Novalis–Vielleicht Bist Du Ein Clown (Novalis) 1978
Nu A Golpe De Latigo (Spain) 1975
Nu Cuentos De Ayer U De Hoy (Spain)
O'Keefe, Danny–Rainbow Girl
Odissea–Odissea (Italy) 1973
Oho–Baltimore

OMD–Architecture And Morality
OMD–Dazzle Ships
Omega–200 Years After The Last War (Hungary) 1974
Omega–Gammapolis (Hungary) 1978
Omega–Omega (Hungary) 1973
Omega–Skyrover(Hungary) 1978
Omega–Odyssey And Oracle
Osanna–Palepoli
Osanna–Landscape Of Life
Outer Limits–A Boy Playing The Magical Bugle
Horn (Japan)
Outer Limits–Misty Moon (Japan)
Outer Limits–The Scene Of Pale Blue (Japan)
P.F.M.–Per Un Amico (Italy) 1972
P.F.M.–Storia Di Un Minuto (Italy) 1972
P.F.M.–Chocolate Kings
P.F.M–Photos Of Ghosts 1973
P.F.M.–When The World Became A World 1975
Pallas–The Wedge (UK)
Paolo Rustichelli/Carlo Bordini Opera Prima (Italy)
Passport–Cross Collateral (Germany)
Passport–Looking Thru (Germany)
Pavlov's Dog–At The Sound Of The Bell (US) 1976
Pavlov's Dog–Pampered Menial (US) 1975
Pell Mell–Marburg (Germany) 1972
Pell Mell–Only A Star (Germany)
Pentwater–Pentwater (US)
Pete Brown & Piblokto–Thousands On A Raft (UK)
Phillips, Anthony–The Geese And The Ghost
Pinder, Michael–The Promise (UK) 1976
Pinder Michael–Of The Shelf (US) 1993
Pink Floyd–Umma Gumma (UK)
Pink Floyd–Julia Dream single (UK) 1968
Pink Floyd–Atom Heart Mother (UK) 1970
Pink Floyd–Saucerful Of Secrets
Planetarium–Infinity (Italy)
Plasticland–Radio Fuzzbox Wig
Popol Vuh–Popol Vuh (Norway)
Popol Vuh–Quiche Maya (Norway)
Popol Vuh -Stolen Through Time (Norway)
Prince–Prince (France)
Pretty Things–SF Sorrow
Procession–Frontiera (Italy)
Pulsar–The Strands Of The Future 1976 (France)
Pulsar–Halloween (France)
Pythagoras–After The Silence 1982
Quatro, Suzi
Quatro, Michael
Quella Vecchia Locanda–Quella Vecchia Locanda (Italy)
Quicksand–Home Is Where I Belong (UK)
Rabbit (Bundrick)–Broken Arrow
Radiomobel–Gudand Garam (Sweden)
Ragnarok–Nooks (New Zealand)
Ragnarok–Ragnarok (New Zealand)
Rainbow–Long Live Rock And Roll
Ramses–La Leyal (Germany) 1975
Raw Material–Insolent Lady (UK)
Raw Material–Time Is (UK)
Reale Academia Di Musica–Reale Academia Di
Muska (Italy)
Reale Academia Di Musica–Vertigine (Italy)
Red Hot Chile Peppers–Mothers Milk
Red Hot Chile Peppers–Blood Sugar Sex Magick
Red Kross–Phaseshifter
Refugee–Refugee (UK) 1974
REM–Green
Renaissance–Arabesque (UK)
Renaissance–Song For All Seasons
Renaissance–Azur d'Or (UK)
Renia–First Offenders
Roberts, Andy–Queen Of The Moonlight World (UK)
Rockhead–Rockhead
Rolling Stones–His Satanic Majesty's Request
Rolling Stones–Beggar's Banquet
Romatic Warriors–Battlefield (Italy)
Roxy Music
Roxy Music–Stranded
Roxy Music–Viva Live
Rundgren, Todd–Todd
Rundgren, Todd–A Wizard, A True Star
Rundgren, Todd–Something, Anything
Rush–2112

Rustichelli I Bordini–Opera Prima (Italy)
S.B.B.–S.B.B. (Poland) 1978
Sahara–Sunrise
Samla Mannas -Mamma Maltid (Sweden)
Sandrose–Sandrose (France) 1973
Sanguiliano–Take Off (Italy)
Santana–Welcome(US)
Saure Britako–Gauzar (Spain) 1978
Schoener, Eberhard–Video Magic
Schicke Fuhrs Frohling–Sunburst (Germany)
Schicke Fuhrs Frohling–Symphonic Pictures (Germany) 1976
Scorpions–Lonesome Crow
Scorpions–Fly To The Rainbow
Scorpions–In Trance
Second Hand–Death May Be Your Santa Claus (UK)
Seger, Bob–The Road (US)
Seventh Wave–Psi Fi (UK) 1975
Seventh Wave–Things To Come (UK) 1974
Shingetsu–Shingetsu (Japan) 1979
Shoot On The Frontier (UK)
Simon Dupree & Big Sound–Kites (UK) 1982
Siouxsie And The Banshees–A Kiss In The Dreamhouse
Skafish
Skin Alley–Skin Alley (UK)
Smak–Crna Dama (Yugoslavia)
Smak–Smak (Yugoslavia)
Small Faces–Small Faces
Small Wonder–1st Album
Smashing Pumpkins–Siamese Dream
Smith, Ernie–Jamaican
Smith, Bob–The Visit (US)
Smithereens–Blowup
Solid Ground–Made In Rock (Sweden)
Spent Poets–Spent Poets
Spirit Of Christmas–Lies To Live By (Canada) 1974
Spring–Spring (UK) 1971
Stackridge–Extravaganza (UK) 1974
Stackridge–Mr. Mick (UK) 1976
Stackridge–Pinafore (UK) 1974
Stafford, Jim–Not Just Another Pretty Foot
Steve Miller Band–Brave New World
Steve Miller Band–In My First Mind
St. Mikael–Claustromania (Sweden)
Stories–Going Underground
Stories–About Us
Strange Advance–Strange Advance
Strange Advance–Strange Advance 2
Strange Advance–The Distance Between
Strawbs–Bursting At The Seams (UK) 1973
Strawbs–From The Witchwood (UK) 1971
Strawbs–Ghosts (UK) 1974
Strawbs–Grave New World (UK) 1972
Strawbs–Hero And Heroine (UK) 1974
Strawbs–Burning For You
Strawbs–Deep Cuts
Strawbs–Dead Lines
Stray–Suicide (UK)
Symphonic Slam–Symphonic Slam (Canada)
Synergy–Electronic Realizations For Rock Orch.. (US)
T2–It'll All Work Out In Bloomland (UK)
T Rex–Tanx (UK)
T Rex–Futuristic Dragon
Talk Talk–The Colour Of Spring
Talk Talk–It's My Mix
Tako–Tako (Yugoslavia)
Tako–U Vreci Za Spavenje (Yugoslavia)
Tangerine Dream–Alpha Centauri (Germany) 1971
Tangerine Dream–Atem (Germany) 1973
Tangerine Dream–Cyclone (Germany) 1978
Tangerine Dream–Encore (Germany) 1977
Tangerine Dream–Force Majeure (Germany) 1979
Tangerine Dream–Live Miles (Germany)
Tangerine Dream–Pargomon (Germany)
Tangerine Dream–Phaedra (Germany) 1974
Tangerine Dream–Ricochet (Germany) 1975
Tangerine Dream–Rubycon (Germany) 1975
Tangerine Dream–Sorcerer (Germany) 1977
Tangerine Dream–Stratosfear (Germany) 1976
Tangerine Dream–Zeit (Germany) 1972
Tango–Tango
Tantra–Mysterioso i Maravilhas
Tantra–Tantra

Taurus–See You Again
Taurus–Illusions Of A Night (Holland)
Taylor, Vic–Whenever I Seem To Be Far Away
Terpandre–Terpandre (France)
Texas–Homer
Theatre–No More Rhymes But Mr. Brainstorm (Italy)
The Enid–Aerie Fairy Nonsense (UK)
The Enid–Something Wicked This Way Comes (UK)
The Fortunes–I Can't Remember Where She Went
The Indians–Indianism (US)
The Moor–Every Pixie Tells A Story (Sweden)
The Move–Blackberry Way (single)
The Move–Curly (single)
The Pretty Things–S.F. Sorrow (UK)
The Trip–The Trip (Italy)
The Undisputed-Truth Earthquake Shake
The Zombies–Odyssey And Oracle (UK)
Thierry Fervant–Seasons Of Life (Switzerland)
Thin Lizzy–1st Album (UK)
Thin Lizzy–Shades Of A Blue Orphanage
30 Years War/Trettioariga Kriget–30 Years War
30 Years War/Trettioariga Kriget–Warsong (Sweden)
Thompson, Richard–Mirror Blue
Thompson, Richard–Rumor And Sigh
Three Man Army–A Third Of A Lifetime (UK)
Tibbets, Steve–1st and 2nd album
Tin–Tin
Tomita–Snowflakes Are Dancing (Japan)
Too Much–Too Much (Japan)
Trace–Trace
Trace–Birds
Traffic–Dear Mr. Fantasy (UK) 1967
Traffic–When The Eagle Flies (UK) 1974
Tranquility–Silver (UK) 1972
Travis–Found Myself In You (UK)
Trettioariga Krige–Krigssang (Sweden) 1973
Twennty Nine Palms–ST
Uncle Green–Book Of Bad Thoughts
Univers Zero–Ceux Du Dehors (Belgium)
Uriah Heep–Very Eavy Very Umble (UK) 1970
Uriah Heep–Uriah Heep
Uriah Heep–Salisbury
Uriah Heep–High And Mighty
Uriah Heep–Return To Fantasy
Van Der Graaf Generator–Pawn Hearts (UK) 1971
Various–Rime Of The Ancient Sampler 1993
Vega Suzanne–99 degrees
Vic. Perainos Kingdom–Come Lady Of The Morning
Vic. Perainos Kingdom–Come No Man's Land (US)
Violent Femmes–Why Do Birds Sing?
Wagner, Adrian–Distances Between Us (UK)
Waits, Tom–Franks Wild Years
Wakeman, Rick–Journey To The Center Of The Earth (UK)
Wakeman, Rick–The Six Wives Of Henry VIII (UK) 1973
Wallenstein–Blitz Krieg(Germany) 1971
Wallenstein–Cosmic Century (Germany) 1973
Wallenstein–Mother Universe (Germany) 1972
Wally–Valley Gardens (UK)
Wally–Wally (UK) 1974
Web–Spider (UK)
Wedge–No One Left But Me
West, Leslie–The Great Fatsby (US)
White Wing–White Wing
Wind–Morning (Germany)
Windchase–1 Symphinity
Windflower–Windflower (US)
Wishbone–Ash Four (UK)
Wonderstuff–Construction For The Modern Idiot
Wonderstuff–Never Loved Elvis
Woolly Wolstenholme–Maestoso (UK) 1980
X–Hey Zeus
XTC–Chips From The Chocolate Fireball 1993
Yanagida, Hiro–Hiro Cosmos 1974
Ybo Ybo–Alienation
Ybo Ybo–Kingdom Of Family Dream (Japan)
Yes–Close To The Edge (UK) 1972
Yes–Fragile (UK) 1971
Yes -Tales From Topographic Oceans(UK) 1975
Yes -The Yes Album (UK) 1971
Yes–Yes Shows (UK)
Yes–Drama
Yes–Relayer

Yes -Union
Yes–Going For The One
Yes–Yessongs
Zauber–Phoenix (Italy) 1992
Zauner, Stefan–Narziss (Germany) 1976
Zebra–Zebra
Zomby Woof–Ridin' On A Tear (Germany)

PART II: From Mellotron Archives Newsletter #7

La Maguina de Hacer Pajaros–La Maguina de Hacer Pajaros 1976
10cc–10cc
10cc–Sheet Music
Now & Then (Germany)–Reflections On The Future
9:30–Fly (U.K.)
A Full Moon Consort–The Men In The Moon 1978 (US)
Absolute Elsewhere–In Search Of Ancient Gods 1976 (UK)
Acqua Fragile–Mass Media Stars
Agitation–II
Agitation–Free 2nd
Ain Soph–A Story Of Mysterious Forest 1980 (Japan)
Albatros–Primo (US)
Ambrosia–Ambrosia
Ambrosia–One Eighty (Chamberlin)
Amon Duul II–Dance Of The Lemmings (Tanz der Lemminge)
Amon Duul II–Pyragony X
Amos, Tori–Upside Down 1992
Arti e Mestieri -Giro di Valzer Par Domani 1975
Arti e Mestieri -Tilt! 1974
Ashra Temple -Starring Rosie 1972
Atonal–Plegaria Urbana 1979 (Argentina)
Badger–The White Ladies 1974
Barclay James Harvest–XII 1978
Bark–Hard
Besombes & Rizet–Pole
Bi Kyo Ran Ran–Live Volume III 1994
Birth Control–Rebirth 1974 (Germany)
Blistering Moments–Therapeutic Dreams
Bo Hanson–Ur Trollkarlen's Hatt 1972 (Sweden)
Bo Hanson–Attic Thoughts 1975 (Sweden)
Bo Hanson–Mallanvasen 1973 (Sweden)
Bo Hanson–The Magician's Hat 1973 (Sweden)
Brown, Arthur–Requiem 1982
Burmer, Richard–Mosaic 1984 (US)
Burmer, Richard–Bakti Point 1987 (US)
Byron, David–Solo LP 1976 (UK)
Canarios–Cycles
Carmen–Dancing On A Cold Wind
Carmen–The Gypsies
Catorze (iu) Bis–Catorze Bis II 1980
Celeste–Celeste 2 1991
Celeste–Celeste Second Plus 1993
Celeste–I Suoni In Una Afara O.S.T. 1974
Celluloid–Jupiter
Celluloid–Mercury 1983
Chac Mool (Mexico)–Nadie en Especial 1980
Cherubin–Cherub Safety Match
City Boy–City Boy
Cosmos Factory–A Journey With The Cosmos Factory 1975
Crack Si Todo Hiciera Crack1979
Cultural Noise–Aphonsims Insane (Sweden)
Curved Air–Second Album 1971
Cybotron–Colossus 1979 (Australia)
Czeslaw Nieman & Aerolit Idee Fixe 198–
Czeslaw Niemen–Mourner's Rhapsody 1975
Dallaylio–Sera Mattina 1972 (Italy)
Danna, Mychael–Elements 1979 (Canada)
Decayes–Accidental Music
Deep Purple–First two records
Dimmornas Bro–Dimmornas Bro 1977 (Sweden)
Dimmornas Bro–Mal 1989 (Sweden)
Dionnel Bregent–... Et Le Troisieme Jour 1975 (Canada)
Dionnel Bregent–Deux 1977 (Canada)
Downes, Geoffrey–The Light Program 1987
Dragon–Kalahen 1977
Dryss–Vision In The Dark 1987 (Switzerland)
Earth Star–Atom Kraft? Nein, Danke! (Birotron)
Eberhard Schoener–Events 1980
Eberhard Schoener–The Book 1978
Eberhard Schoener–Trance-Formation 1977
Eberhard Schoener–Video Flashback 1979

Eela Craig–Hats Of Glass 1977 (Austria)
Eela Craig–One Niter 1976 (Austria)
Egg–Egg
Egg–The Polite Force 1971
Ekseotuib–Ekseption '78 1978
Ekseption–Dance Macabre 1981
Eloiteran–Lost Paradise 1981 (Switzerland)
Embryo Rache–Steig Aus
Embryo–Surfin' (Germany)
Emergency–No Compromise
Eroc–Eroc 1975 (Germany)
Eroc–Zwei 1976 (Germany)
Family Music–In A Dolls House 1968
Far East Family Band–Nipponjin 1975
Far East Family Band–Parallel World 1975
Far East Family Band–Tenkujin 1978
Finch–Beyond Expression 1976
Fireballet–Night On Bald Mountain 1975 (US)
Flyte–Dawn Dancer (Belgium)
Galahad–Nothing Is Written 1991
Galdalf–Visions 1981 (Austria)
Gandalf–To Another Horizon 1983 (Austria)
Gandalf–Fantasia 1986 (Austria)
Gandalf–Journey To An Imaginary Land 1980 (Austria)
Gandalf–Magic Theatre 1983 (Austria)
Gandalf–More Than Just A Seagull 1984 (Austria)
Gandalf–Tales From A Long-Forgotten Kingdom 1984 (Austria)
Gandalf–The Shining 1985 (Austria)
Gandalf–The Universal Play 1987 (Austria)
Gandalf–Various LP's 1982-1993 (Austria)
Genesis–And Then There Were Three... 1978
Genesis–Seconds Out
Geodesium–Double Eclipse 1981 (Sweden)
Geodesium–Geodesium 1977 (Sweden)
Gerard–Irony Of Fate 1991
Gila–Bury My Heart At Wounded Knee
Giles, Giles & Fripp 1967 (UK)
Giles, Giles & Fripp–The Cheerful Insanity Of...
Glider–Glider (US)
Gracious–Once Upon A Windy Day (single)
Hancock, Herbie–Crossing 1972
Haris Chalkitis–Haris Chalkitis 1976 (Greece)
Heldon–Heldon IV
Hoelderlin–Hoelderlin 1975 (Germany)
Hoelderlin–Holderlin's Traum 1972 (Germany)
Hootenanny Singers–Dan Andersson Pa Vart Satt (Sweden)
Howe, Steve–Beginnings 1975 (UK)
Hugh Cornnell & Rbt Williams–Nosferatu
I Pooh–Un Po' del Nostro Tempo Migliore
Iceberg–Tutankhamon 1975 (Spain)
ID–Where Are We Going
Illusion Enchanted–Caress 1990
IQ–Ever
IQ–Living Proof 1986
IQ–Nomzamo 1987
IQ–Nine In A Pond Is Here (UK)
Isao Tomita–Bolero/ Daphnis and Chloe 1980
Isao Tomita–Firebird Suite 1976
Isao Tomita–Kosmos 1978
Isao Tomita–Pictures At An Exhibition 1975
Isao Tomita–Space Waltz 1984
Isao Tomita–The Bermuda Triangle 1979
Isao Tomita–The Grand Canyon 1982
Isao Tomita–The Planets 1976
Isildurs Bane–Isildurs Bane 1984 (Sweden)
Isildurs Bane–Sea Reflections 1985 (Sweden)
Jadis–More Than Meets The Eye
Jean Michael Jarre–Equinox 1987
Julian Jay Savarin–Waiters On The Dance
Julian's–Treatment (UK) 2nd LP 1973
Jun Fukamachi–The Tale Of The Heike 1978 (Japan)
Kaipa–Stockholm Symphonie
Kaipa–Inget Nytt Under Solen 1976
Kaipa–Solo 1978
Kangaroo Kourt–Messages In Ether
Karat–Albatros (E. Germany)
Karat–Ueber Sieben Bruecken (E. Germany)
Keats–Keats 1984 (US)
Kerrs Pink–Kong Eduards/Feberliten single 1979 (Norway)
King Crimson–Earthbound 1972 (UK)
Kitaro–Kitaro In Person 1980

Kitaro–Silk Road I 1980
Kitaro–Silk Road II 1980
Kitaro–Silk Road III 1981
Lazza Riskouski–Roses For A General 1984 (Yugoslavia)
Le Orme–In Concerto 1974
Lift–Lift 1977 (E. Germany)
Lily–VCU (Germany)
Lodge–Smell Of A Friend 1988
Lutz Rahn–Solo Trip 1978 (Germany)
Machiavel–Jester
Madison Dyke–Zeitmaschine 1977 (Germany)
Magma–Attahk (Chamberlin)
Mahaujin–Babylonia Suite 1978
Mako–In Other Regions 1986
Manticore–Time To Fly 1984 (Sweden)
Marillion–Forgotten Songs (UK)
Marz–The Dream Is Over
McCartney, Paul–Flowers In The Dirt 1989
McPhee, Tony–The Two Sides Of...) 1972
Mind Over Matter–Music For Paradise 1986 (Germany)
Message–The Dawn Anew Is Coming
Metcalf, Thomas–One 1989 (US)
Move–The Best Of The Move
Muyen–The Princess Of Kingdom Come 1988
Mythos–Concrete City 1978
Mythos–Quasar 1980
Nektar–A Tab In The Ocean 1972
Nektar–Down To Earth
Nine Days Wonder–Only The Dancers
Nine Days Wonder-We Never Lost Control
Nouva Idea–Clowns 1971 (Italy)
Nouva Idea–In The Beginning 1970 (Italy)
Nouva Idea–Mr. E. Jones 1972 (Italy)
Novalis–Wer Schmetterlinge Lachen Hort 1978
Novela–Novela (Niwakugeni) 1980 (Japan)
Nuvole di Paylis–And Then 1994 (Italy)
Octopus–The Boat Of Thoughts 1976 (Germany)
Omega–8 Csillagor Utjan 1978
Omega–9 Gammapolis 1978
Omega–Omega 1975 (English)
Omega–Omega III 1974 (English)
Omega–7 Idorablo 1977 (Hungarian)
Osamu Kitajjima–Osamu 1973 (Japan)
Outer Limits–Indian Collection 1988
Outer Limits–Made In Japan Sampler –side two 1981
Outer Limits–Marionette's Lament 1987
Outer Limits–Outer Mania 1994
Pallas–Arrive Alive 1981
Pallas–Eyes In The Night 1984
Pallas–The Pallas Tape 1981
Pallas–The Sentinel 1984
Paradis, Vanessa
Passport–Handmade 1973
Pazzo FanFano diMusica–Pazzo FanFano di Musica 1989 (Japan)
PFM–L'Isola di Niente
Phantom–Phantom's Divine Comedy (Germany)
Pink Floyd "Embryo" from Works 1983
Popol Ace–Popol Ace 1973
Popol Ace–Curly Sounds 1978
Qualla Vacchia Locanda–Il Tempo Della Gioia 1974
Qualla Vacchia Locanda–Live 1994
Rainbow Theatre–The Armada 1975 (Australia)
Ramses–Eternity Rise
Ray Manzarek–The Golden Scarab 1975
Ray Manzarek–The Whole Thing Started With Rock N Roll 1973
Reinhard Lakomy–Das Geheime Leben 1981 (E. Germany)
Release Music Orchestra–Beyond The Limit 1977 (Germany)
Release Music Orchestra–Garuda 1975 (Ger)
Release Music Orchestra–Get The Ball 1976 (Ger)
Release Music Orchestra–Life 1974 (Ger)
Release Music Orchestra–News 1979 (Ger)
Return To Forever–Live The Complete Concert 1978
Rosalia–Zillion Tears 1990 (Japan)
Rousseau–Flower In Asphalt 1985 (Germany)
Rundgren, Todd–Initiation
Sab–Crystallization 1978 (Japan)
Sadistic Mika Band–Black Ship (2nd album)
Samla mammas manna–Snorugarnas Symfoni (Sweden)
SBB–Follow My Dream 1978
SBB–Welcome 1979
SBB–Za Slowem Siegne Do Ciebie 1977

Scherpanzeal, Ton–Le Carnaval Des Animaux 1975 (Holland)
Sense Of Wonder–Shingenma Teisen 1984 (Japan)
Sergius Golowin–Lord Krishna von Goloka
Shine Dion–Berkana 1994 (Norway)
Shylock–Ile de Fievre (France)
Skrzek, Jozef–Pamietnik Karoling 1978 (Poland)
Sky Cries Mary–Return To The Inner Experience
Social Tension–It Reminds Me Of Those Days (Japan)
Soundgarden–Super Unknown
Space Art–Trip To The Head Center 1978 (France)
Spada, Tony–Balance Of Power 1992 (US)
Split Enz–Beginning Of The Enz
Split Enz–Mental Notes
Split Enz–Second Thoughts
Strangers On A Train (UK)–The Key Part II: The Labyrinth 1993
Strangers On A Train (UK)–The Key: The Prophecy 1990
Sway–Human Carnage 1979 (Belgium)
Synchestra–Mother Earth's Lullaby 1981 (US)
Tantra–Holocausto
Taurus–Works 1976-1981 1990
Ten CC–Ten CC 1972 (England)
Terje Rypdal–Whenever I Seem Far Away 1974
Terraced Garden–Melody & Menace 1982 (Canada)
The Bonzo Dog Band–The Doughnut In Granny's
Greenhouse 1968 (UK)
The Trip–Atlantide 1972
The Trip–Caronte 1971
Torn Curtain
Tace–The White Ladies 1976
Tritonus–Tritonus 1975 (Germany)
True Myth–1st LP 1967 (Canada)
Twenty Sixty Six And Then Reflections–On The Future
Twenty Sixty Six And then Reflections!
Uggla, Magnus–Om Bobbo Viking (Sweden)
Utopia
Utopia–(Germany)
Van der Graaf Generator–World Record
Van der Graaf Generator–Still Life 1976
Wakeman, Rick–The Myths And Legends of King Arthur... 1975
Wakeman, Rick–No Earthly Connection 1976
Wakeman, Rick–White Rock 1976
Wakeman, Rick–Criminal Record 1975
Wallenstein–Stories, Songs And Symphonies 1975
When–Death In Blue Lake (Norway)
White Noise–An Electric Storm 1969 (UK)
Wilson, Andrew Thomas–The Chain Reaction 1980
White Willow–Ignus Fautus 1994 (Norway)
Woodorffe, Jezz–Opposite Directions 1980 (England)
XTC–Mummer
XTC–Skylarking (Chamberlin)
Yes–Yesterdays 1975 (UK)
Yonin Bayashi–Ishomu shomuhatsu 1974 (Japan)

Sources and Further Reading

Dunn, Brian and Korb, Jerry (1997). *8 Seconds at a Time (The Mellotron Story), Have You Heard* magazine, Issues # 11 (4-5) & 12 (2-3)

Mellotron Archives/David Kean
111 Lake Wapta Rise. SE
Calgary AB, T2J-2N1 CANADA
phone: (403) 262-2121/fax: (403) 266-5145
email: **mellod@netwood.net**
website: **http://www.mellotron.com**

Streetly Electronics/John Bradley and Martin Smith
1 Rose Cottages, Uttoxeter Road
Blithbury, Rugeley, Staffordshire, WS15 3HU
phone: 01889 504211
email: **TRONBROS@aol.com**
website: **http://members.aol.com/tronpage**

Other Mellotron websites of interest:

The Bomb Factory:
http://www.bombfactory.com
King Crimson's Mellotrons:
http://www.dcrp.ced.berkeley.edu/cervero/crimtron.htm
Norm Leete's Mellotron Page:
http://members.aol.com/tronpage
Mellotrons, Chamberlins, and Their Sounds:
http://www.geocities.com/SunsetStrip/Studio/7846/mtron.html
Ken Merbler's Mellotron:
http://photomail.filmworks.com/sharing/roll.asp?Key=0734116663060008
http://www.tronsounds.com
http://www.crosswinds.net/~kenmerb
Ken Leonard's Mellotron Page:
http://www.kleonard.com
Mike Dickson's Mellotron Samples:
http://blackcat.demon.co.uk/tron/samples.htm
Pierre Veilleux's Mellotrons:
http://perso.wanadoo.fr/egrefin
The Ultimate Mellotron Recording List:
http://freespace.virgin.net/andy.thompson
Mark Glinsky's Keyboards:
http://www.magicnet.net/~mglnsky/msgkeys.html
Don Tillman's page:
http://www.till.com/articles/Mellotron/index.html
Sarah Angliss' page:
http://www.mongrelmedia.co.uk/sarahpages/sarahmellotron.htm

More Mellotron pictures and samples:

http://www.enteract.com/~yumyum/index.html
http://h002078cbccbd.ne.mediaone.net/tronsounds